Gabriel García Márquez

HISPANICS OF ACHIEVEMENT

Gabriel García Márquez

Sean Dolan

CHELSEA HOUSE PUBLISHERS

PHILADELPHIA

CHELSEA HOUSE PUBLISHERS

Editorial Director: Richard Rennert
Executive Managing Editor: Karyn Gullen Browne
Executive Editor: Sean Dolan
Copy Chief: Robin James
Picture Editor: Adrian G. Allen
Art Director: Robert Mitchell
Manufacturing Director: Gerald Levine
Systems Manager: Lindsey Ottman
Production Coordinator: Marie Claire Cebrián-Ume

HISPANICS OF ACHIEVEMENT
Senior Editor: Philip Koslow

Staff for *GABRIEL GARCÍA MÁRQUEZ*
Associate Editor: David Carter
Copy Editor: Laura Petermann
Designer: M. Cambraia Magalhaes
Picture Researcher: Wendy P. Wills
Cover Illustration: Daniel Mark Duffy

5 7 9 8 6 4

Library of Congress Cataloging-in-Publication Data
Dolan, Sean.
Gabriel García Márquez / Sean Dolan.
p. cm.—(Hispanics of achievement)
Includes bibliographical references and index.
Summary: Discusses the life and career of the Colombian novelist who achieved fame in a genre known as magical realism and who won the 1982 Nobel Prize for Literature.
ISBN 0-7910-1243-3
0-7910-1270-0 (pbk.)
1. García Márquez, Gabriel, 1928– —Juvenile literature. 2. Authors, Colombian—20th century—Biography—Juvenile literature. [1. García Márquez, Gabriel, 1928– . 2. Authors, Colombian.] I. Title. II. Series.
PQ8180.17.A73Z655 1993
93-9478
863—dc20
CIP
[B]
AC

CONTENTS

HISPANICS OF ACHIEVEMENT

JOAN BAEZ
Mexican-American folksinger

RUBÉN BLADES
Panamanian lawyer and entertainer

JORGE LUIS BORGES
Argentine writer

PABLO CASALS
Spanish cellist and conductor

MIGUEL DE CERVANTES
Spanish writer

CESAR CHAVEZ
Mexican-American labor leader

JULIO CÉSAR CHÁVEZ
Mexican boxing champion

EL CID
Spanish military leader

HENRY CISNEROS
Mexican-American political leader

ROBERTO CLEMENTE
Puerto Rican baseball player

SALVADOR DALÍ
Spanish painter

PLÁCIDO DOMINGO
Spanish singer

GLORIA ESTEFAN
Cuban-American singer

GABRIEL GARCÍA MÁRQUEZ
Colombian writer

FRANCISCO JOSÉ DE GOYA
Spanish painter

JULIO IGLESIAS
Spanish singer

RAUL JULIA
Puerto Rican actor

FRIDA KAHLO
Mexican painter

JOSÉ MARTÍ
Cuban revolutionary and poet

RITA MORENO
Puerto Rican singer and actress

PABLO NERUDA
Chilean poet and diplomat

OCTAVIO PAZ
Mexican poet and critic

PABLO PICASSO
Spanish artist

ANTHONY QUINN
Mexican-American actor

DIEGO RIVERA
Mexican painter

LINDA RONSTADT
Mexican-American singer

ANTONIO LÓPEZ DE SANTA ANNA
Mexican general and politician

GEORGE SANTAYANA
Spanish philosopher and poet

JUNÍPERO SERRA
Spanish missionary and explorer

LEE TREVINO
Mexican-American golfer

PANCHO VILLA
Mexican revolutionary

CHELSEA HOUSE PUBLISHERS

HISPANICS OF ACHIEVEMENT

Rodolfo Cardona

The Spanish language and many other elements of Spanish culture are present in the United States today and have been since the country's earliest beginnings. Some of these elements have come directly from the Iberian Peninsula; others have come indirectly, by way of Mexico, the Caribbean basin, and the countries of Central and South America.

Spanish culture has influenced America in many subtle ways, and consequently many Americans remain relatively unaware of the extent of its impact. The vast majority of them recognize the influence of Spanish culture in America, but they often do not realize the great importance and long history of that influence. This is partly because Americans have tended to judge the Hispanic influence in the United States in statistical terms rather than to look closely at the ways in which individual Hispanics have profoundly affected American culture. For this reason, it is fitting that Americans obtain more than a passing acquaintance with the origins of these Spanish cultural elements and gain an understanding of how they have been woven into the fabric of American society.

It is well documented that Spanish seafarers were the first to explore and colonize many of the early territories of what is today called the United States of America. For this reason, students of geography discover Hispanic names all over the map of the United States. For instance, the Strait of Juan de Fuca was named after the Spanish explorer who first navigated the waters of the Pacific Northwest; the names of states such as Arizona (arid zone), Montana (mountain), Florida (thus named because it was reached on Easter Sunday, which in Spanish is called the feast of Pascua Florida), and California (named after a fictitious land in one of the first and probably the most popular among the Spanish novels of chivalry, *Amadis of Gaul*) are all derived from Spanish; and there are numerous mountains, rivers, canyons, towns, and cities with Spanish names throughout the United States.

Not only explorers but many other illustrious figures in Spanish history have helped define American culture. For example, the 13th-century king of Spain, Alfonso X, also known as the Learned, may be unknown to the majority of Americans, but his work on the codification of Spanish law has greatly influenced the evolution of American law, particularly in the jurisdictions of the Southwest. For this contribution a statue of him stands in the rotunda of the Capitol in Washington, D.C. Likewise, the name Diego Rivera may be unfamiliar to most Americans, but this Mexican painter influenced many American artists whose paintings, commissioned during the Great Depression and the New Deal era of the 1930s, adorn the walls of government buildings throughout the United States. In recent years the contributions of Puerto Ricans, Mexicans, Mexican Americans (Chicanos), and Cubans in American cities such as Boston, Chicago, Los Angeles, Miami, Minneapolis, New York, and San Antonio have been enormous.

The importance of the Spanish language in this vast cultural complex cannot be overstated. Spanish, after all, is second only to English as the most widely spoken of Western languages within the United States as well as in the entire world. The popularity of the Spanish language in America has a long history.

In addition to Spanish exploration of the New World, the great Spanish literary tradition served as a vehicle for bringing the language and culture to America. Interest in Spanish literature in America began when English immigrants brought with them translations of Spanish masterpieces of the Golden Age. As early as 1683, private libraries in Philadelphia and Boston contained copies of the first picaresque novel, *Lazarillo de Tormes*, translations of Francisco de Quevedo's *Los Sueños*, and copies of the immortal epic of reality and illusion *Don Quixote*, by the great Spanish writer Miguel de Cervantes. It would not be surprising if Cotton Mather, the arch-Puritan, read *Don Quixote* in its original Spanish, if only to enrich his vocabulary in preparation for his writing *La fe del cristiano en 24 artículos de la Institución de Cristo, enviada a los españoles para que abran sus ojos* (The Christian's Faith in 24 Articles of the Institution of Christ, Sent to the Spaniards to Open Their Eyes), published in Boston in 1699.

Over the years, Spanish authors and their works have had a vast influence on American literature—from Washington Irving, John Steinbeck, and Ernest Hemingway in the novel to Henry Wadsworth Longfellow and Archibald MacLeish in poetry. Such important American writers as James Fenimore Cooper, Edgar Allan Poe, Walt Whitman, Mark Twain, and Herman Melville all owe a sizable debt to the Spanish literary tradition. Some writers, such as Willa Cather and Maxwell Anderson, who explored Spanish themes they came into contact with in the American Southwest and Mexico, were influenced less directly but no less profoundly.

Important contributions to a knowledge of Spanish culture in the United States were also made by many lesser known individuals—teachers, publishers, historians, entrepreneurs, and others—with a love for Spanish culture. One of the most significant of these contributions was made by Abiel Smith, a Harvard College graduate of the class of 1764, when he bequeathed stock worth $20,000 to Harvard for the support of a professor of French and Spanish. By 1819 this endowment had produced enough income to appoint a professor, and the philologist and humanist George Ticknor became the first holder of the Abiel

Smith Chair, which was the very first endowed Chair at Harvard University. Other illustrious holders of the Smith Chair would include the poets Henry Wadsworth Longfellow and James Russell Lowell.

A highly respected teacher and scholar, Ticknor was also a collector of Spanish books, and as such he made a very special contribution to America's knowledge of Spanish culture. He was instrumental in amassing for Harvard libraries one of the first and most impressive collections of Spanish books in the United States. He also had a valuable personal collection of Spanish books and manuscripts, which he bequeathed to the Boston Public Library.

With the creation of the Abiel Smith Chair, Spanish language and literature courses became part of the curriculum at Harvard, which also went on to become the first American university to offer graduate studies in Romance languages. Other colleges and universities throughout the United States gradually followed Harvard's example, and today Spanish language and culture may be studied at most American institutions of higher learning.

No discussion of the Spanish influence in the United States, however brief, would be complete without a mention of the Spanish influence on art. Important American artists such as John Singer Sargent, James A. M. Whistler, Thomas Eakins, and Mary Cassatt all explored Spanish subjects and experimented with Spanish techniques. Virtually every serious American artist living today has studied the work of the Spanish masters as well as the great 20th-century Spanish painters Salvador Dalí, Joan Miró, and Pablo Picasso.

The most pervasive Spanish influence in America, however, has probably been in music. Compositions such as Leonard Bernstein's *West Side Story*, the Latinization of William Shakespeare's *Romeo and Juliet* set in New York's Puerto Rican quarter, and Aaron Copland's *Salon Mexico* are two obvious examples. In general, one can hear the influence of Latin rhythms—from tango to mambo, from guaracha to salsa—in virtually every form of American music.

This series of biographies, which Chelsea House has published under the general title HISPANICS OF ACHIEVEMENT, constitutes further recognition of—and a renewed effort to bring forth to the consciousness of America's young people—the contributions that Hispanic people have made not only in the United States but throughout the civilized world. The men and women who are featured in this series have attained a high level of accomplishment in their respective fields of endeavor and have made a permanent mark on American society.

The title of this series must be understood in its broadest possible sense: The term *Hispanics* is intended to include Spaniards, Spanish Americans, and individuals from many countries whose language and culture have either direct or indirect Spanish origins. The names of many of the people included in this series will be immediately familiar; others will be less recognizable. All, however, have attained recognition within their own countries, and often their fame has transcended their borders.

The series HISPANICS OF ACHIEVEMENT thus addresses the attainments and struggles of Hispanic people in the United States and seeks to tell the stories of individuals whose personal and professional lives in some way reflect the larger Hispanic experience. These stories are exemplary of what human beings can accomplish, often against daunting odds and by extraordinary personal sacrifice, where there is conviction and determination. Fray Junípero Serra, the 18th-century Spanish Franciscan missionary, is one such individual. Although in very poor health, he devoted the last 15 years of his life to the foundation of missions throughout California—then a mostly unsettled expanse of land—in an effort to bring a better life to Native Americans through the cultivation of crafts and animal husbandry. An example from recent times, the Mexican-American labor leader Cesar Chavez has battled bitter opposition and made untold personal sacrifices in his effort to help poor agricultural workers who have been exploited for decades on farms throughout the Southwest.

The talent with which each one of these men and women may have been endowed required dedication and hard work to develop and become fully realized. Many of them have enjoyed rewards for their efforts during their own lifetime, whereas others have died poor and unrecognized. For some it took a long time to achieve their goals, for others success came at an early age, and for still others the struggle continues. All of them, however, stand out as people whose lives have made a difference, whose achievements we need to recognize today and should continue to honor in the future.

Gabriel García Márquez

THE CAVE OF THE MAFIA

M any years later, after his book had been universally acclaimed a masterpiece; after it had been translated from Spanish into 26 other languages; after it had won for its author the Nobel Prize for literature and left him rich and so influential in the Spanish-speaking world that Fidel Castro called him the "most powerful man in Latin America," Gabriel García Márquez was to remember the moment during that distant afternoon on the road to Acapulco from Mexico City when he suddenly understood how to translate the words his characters had been speaking to him for so many years.

Later, he would refer to that time as "when I was happy and unknown," but this was nostalgia, for he was then living days of disillusionment. He was almost 37 years old, and 10 years of wandering in the Old World had taken him far from his native Colombia until his settlement in Mexico City with his wife and two sons. The three goals he had established for himself upon graduating from secondary school were yet to be achieved. "I wanted to be a journalist, I wanted to write novels, and I wanted to do something for a more just society," he had decided then, and he was

Gabriel García Márquez, the winner of the 1982 Nobel Prize for literature and one of the 20th century's most acclaimed authors, was 37 years old when he wrote the book that catapulted him to world fame, One Hundred Years of Solitude.

15

satisfied now only with his efforts concerning the first
of these desires. The novel, two novellas, and score of
short stories he had completed since were more criti-
cally acclaimed than read—none of his books had sold
more than 700 copies, and he had never earned a
royalty check—and he had repudiated the published
version of the novel, *La mala hora* (In Evil Hour),
because of unauthorized editorial changes made to it.
Some of the short stories, he had long known, "were
simply intellectual elaborations, nothing to do with
my reality," and he had published the longer works
only at the insistence of his friends. He had little
money, time, or influence to contribute toward the
goal of social justice. "For a long time, of course, things
did not work out for me—almost the first 40 years,"
he said in 1988, speaking without nostalgia. "I had
financial problems; I had work problems. I had not
made it as a writer or anything else. It was a difficult
time emotionally and psychologically; I had the idea
that I was like an extra, that I did not count anywhere." For four years, since 1961, he had completed
no literary work at all. "I'll never write again," he
sadly and repeatedly told his friends.

For 16 years, ever since he had taken a train trip
with his mother to his birthplace of Aracataca in order
to sell the house he had grown up in, García Márquez
had been thinking about a village named Macondo. It
had the same name as a banana plantation near Aracataca that he had known as a child and seen once
again from the windows of his train, and it was the
name he had then assigned to the fictional village
where he hoped to set the great novel he wished so
desperately to write: A history of Macondo—as re-
vealed through the lives of several generations of its
founding family, the Buendías—that would serve as a
"metaphor for Latin America." Several times he had
tried to write that book, and several times he had

Carlos Fuentes, the eminent Mexican novelist, declared García Márquez "a master" after he read the first three chapters of One Hundred Years of Solitude. *García Márquez's novel, published in 1967, sold 30 million copies in 20 years and sparked a worldwide enthusiasm for contemporary Latin American literature.*

failed. The first novella he wrote, *La hojarasca* (Leaf Storm), was set in Macondo, as were several of his short stories, and his other fiction contained allusions to the town and its inhabitants. But for all his accomplishment, these works were nothing more than promising beginnings, hints and glimmers of the world he was trying to create. Though he could see the characters who lived there, especially Colonel Aureliano Buendía, fighter in an eternal civil war, and hear their voices—"I spoke the lines of the people ... for years before writing the book," he would later say—he could not figure out how to tell their story, how to conjure up their world, and he had begun to fear that he never would.

It came to him in January 1965 as he drove with his family in a tiny Opel on the highway from Mexico City to Acapulco. Suddenly, he could hear in his mind every word of the novel, and he understood that the often fantastic events of the book had to be narrated with the same kind of matter-of-fact certainty with which his grandmother had told the little boy she was raising that if he moved from the chair where he was sitting, the ghost of his uncle would emerge from the room opposite and get him. It was a moment of pure artistic inspiration, as rare as an emerald: "All of a sudden—I don't know why—I had this illumination as to how to write the book. I had the tone, everything." To his wife he explained that their vacation at the seashore would have to wait, then he turned the Opel around and headed back for Mexico City. "It was so ripe in me that I could have dictated the first chapter word-by-word to a typist," he remembered later. That chapter began with the famous sentence "Many years later, as he faced the firing squad, Colonel Aureliano Buendía was to remember that distant afternoon when his father took him to discover ice" and told the story of how the gypsies visited Macondo, an isolated "village of twenty adobe houses, built on the bank of a river of clear water that ran along a bed of polished stones," at a time when "the world was so recent that many things lacked names, and in order to indicate them it was necessary to point."

For 18 months of solitude García Márquez labored every day in his room, which his friends took to calling the Cave of the Mafia, while Mercedes, his wife, took over the business of providing for the family. "I had a family—a wife and two small sons— and I had been supporting them by working in public relations and fixing up movie scripts. All that had to cease so I could write my book. But we had no income, so I pawned our car and gave Mercedes the money. From then on, Mercedes had to be like the woman in the Colombian civil wars: She had to run the household and keep life going while I campaigned.

"She performed all kinds of wondrous feats. Every day, somehow, she made sure I had my cigarettes, paper, everything I needed to write. She borrowed money. She got credit from stores. When the book was finished, it turned out that we owed the butcher some 5,000 pesos—which was an enormous sum. Somehow the word had gotten around the neighborhood that I was writing a very important book, and all the shopkeepers wanted to collaborate." The televi-

A view of Mexico City, where García Márquez lived when he began work on One Hundred Years of Solitude. *Following a stroke of inspiration, García Márquez secluded himself in his home and completed the book in 18 months, working every day without a break.*

sion set, the radio, the wall clock, a blender, and finally Mercedes' hair drier—all joined the Opel at the pawnshop.

After a year of work in the Cave of the Mafia, García Márquez sent the first three chapters of his book to Carlos Fuentes, the eminent Mexican novelist. "I have just read eighty pages by a master," Fuentes declared in the pages of *Siempre!*, Mexico's journal of intellectual affairs, after reading about the afternoon Aureliano Buendía's father brought him to discover ice, and the gypsies who come to Macondo to peddle their Old World gadgets and trinkets, and José Arcadio Buendía's quest to solve the alchemists' riddle and his failed journey "through a universe of grief" to find the sea, and the birth of his two sons, the "protomale" José Arcadio and the clairvoyant Aureliano, who "had wept in his mother's womb and been born with his eyes open"; the founding of Macondo, "a truly happy village where no one was over thirty years of age and where no one had died," as the consequence of a pirate's raid and a virgin's fears and a murder over a cockfight; José Arcadio's departure with the gypsies, the onset of the insomnia plague and the loss of memory, and the resurrection of Melquíades, "a heavy gypsy with an untamed beard and sparrow hands" who could not bear the solitude of death; and the arrival of the representative of the central government, who sows the seeds of civil war.

Within a short time, excerpts from the work in progress were published to great acclaim in Colombia, Peru, and France. A publishing house in Buenos Aires, Argentina, arranged with García Márquez to reprint some of his earlier works and to publish his new novel when he finished it, in a first print run of 8,000 copies—a huge number for an author whose combined sales of his four previous books totaled less than half of that. The writer urged caution, but his editor told him not to worry: Favorable word-of-mouth had all but assured him a succès d'estime, and the publisher was certain that the book would sell out its run in several months, with small but steady sales thereafter.

By the summer of 1966, the book was almost finished. Its writing had become a delight, and García Márquez, though nearly poisoned with nicotine (he smoked six packs of cigarettes a day in the Cave of the Mafia), was filled with a feeling of exultation, a sense that "nobody could stop it, that I could do anything I wanted with it, that the book was in the bag." He was experiencing that "perfect correspondence between you and the subject you're working on" that is his definition of artistic inspiration and constitutes the "greatest joy one can have, the best moment." He wrote himself and his friends into his novel's final pages as characters, and Mercedes, too, "a girl with the stealthy beauty of a serpent of the Nile ... the secret girlfriend of Gabriel." There remained only the task of naming it. When he had first thought of and tried to write the book, he called it *La casa* (The House), because it was to take place completely in the Buendías' sprawling home, but that was no longer the case, although the action was confined almost exclusively to Macondo. The new title—*Cien años de soledad* (One Hundred Years of Solitude)—came to him as he was writing the novel's final words. Though the chronicle of six generations of the Buendías encompasses more than a century, the title, with its suggestion of unbearable isolation and inescapable fate, nonetheless evokes perfectly the sad destiny of the family and Macondo, both of them condemned by geography, history, and character to a solitude that is personal, collective, and eternal. With the declaration that "races condemned to one hundred years of solitude did not have a second opportunity on earth," García Márquez ended his novel.

"But when it was done," he would later remember, "we still had problems. Once, toward the end of it all, the typist who had the only copies of many of the chapters of the book was hit by a bus. So the only copies of half the book went flying all over a Mexico City street. Fortunately, the bus didn't kill her, and she was able to get up and reassemble the manuscript." When it was time to mail off the completed manuscript to the publisher, the author did not even have enough money for postage. He sent the first half, and the rest followed after Mercedes pawned some more household implements. One great uncertainty remained: "And what if, after all this, it's a bad novel?"

The Peruvian writer Mario Vargas Llosa called One Hundred Years of Solitude *"one of the rare instances among major, contemporary literary works that can be read, understood, and enjoyed by all."*

Mercedes asked her husband. But García Márquez had a notion that he had created a masterpiece.

The first edition of *One Hundred Years of Solitude* was published in June 1967. Within one week, the entire initial print run—8,000 copies—had sold out at the subway station newsstands where it was distributed. Subsequent runs sold out at a rate of one per week. Over the next three years, *One Hundred Years of Solitude* sold 500,000 copies in Latin America; 20 years after its release, it had sold 10 million copies in the Hispanic world and 30 million copies worldwide, achieving for its author a level of popular success unknown by any other modern writer of Spanish. Its critical reception was, if possible, even more wildly enthusiastic. Peru's preeminent novelist, Mario Vargas Llosa, wrote:

> Perhaps the most mysterious of its virtues is . . . its unlimited accessibility; that is, its power to be within anyone's reach, with distinct but abundant rewards for everyone: for the intelligent reader and the imbecile; for those with a complex mind and for those with a simple one; for the refined who relish prose, contemplate structure and decode the symbols of a story, and for the impatient, who only respond to a crude anecdote. . . . *One Hundred Years of Solitude* is one of the rare instances among major, contemporary literary works that can be read, understood, and enjoyed by all.

Readers in Latin America recognized at once in the history of Macondo—an enchanting village that is home to much misery—and the lives of the Buendías the contradictory, tragic, comical, fantastic, and wonderful reality of their region's past and their own day-to-day existence. Though the novel García Márquez conjured up in the Cave of the Mafia is on one level a profoundly sad one, filled with tragedy and deeply skeptical of the possibility of progress for Latin America, it is a tale told joyfully, in long paragraphs of clear, shimmering prose. Macondo is a world where terrible things happen—human indifference, plagues, civil war, the murder of sons and husbands, massacres, hurricanes, floods, governmental and military oppression, colonial exploitation—but where the miraculous is real. Its inhabitants often behave foolishly or badly, but they are redeemed by their vitality and humanity; though a curious sense of fate prevails throughout, by means of the author's mastery of language—"the only instrument a writer has to use"—the reader cannot help but feel that, as the unnamed protagonist of García Márquez's earlier novella *El coronel no tiene quien le escriba* (No One Writes to the Colonel) puts it, "Life is the best thing that's ever been invented." And as an example of compelling storytelling—a sheer expression of the powers of the imagination—*One Hundred Years of Solitude* stands alone and reveals its creator as a master. "Every page is rammed full of life beyond the capacity of any single reader to absorb," Harold Bloom, the influential North American literary critic, has written.

The novel is at once family saga, myth, fable, fairy tale, parable, bawdy bedroom farce, Rabelaisian satire, realistic recreation of Latin America's past, metaphor for the region's history, and contemplation of its future, and as such was seized on immediately by readers in Latin America, who made Macondo one of the most beloved villages in all of literature, the Buendías one of the most beloved families, and *One Hundred Years of Solitude* one of the most beloved books. According to Vargas Llosa, it created nothing less than a "literary earthquake."

This is us, its readers in Latin America seemed to say, this is our past, and this is our present, and here, at last, is our literature. Ron Arias, a novelist and journalist, was "riding a crowded bus one day in Caracas, [Venezuela,] and two women who looked like secretaries on their lunch break were laughing over certain episodes they'd read in *Cien años de soledad*. I joined in; then it seemed half the bus did. This was in 1969 and it was the year's best seller. Everyone who had read it was bringing up his or her favorite character, and we were all howling together. The book as a whole had struck a common chord with us all, since historically we had all come from Macondo." The author himself, while visiting Cuba in the early 1970s, was asked by a group of peasants what he did for a living. "I write," he answered. "What do you write?" they asked. "I wrote a book called *Cien años de soledad*," he said. "Macondo!" they shouted out gleefully in unison. For other Latin American writers, *One Hundred Years of Solitude* served to prove what they had long been saying—that the contemporary literature of their region was the most exciting and meaningful being produced anywhere in the world. At least so far as literature was concerned, García Márquez had freed Latin America from its solitude. "The great American novel," proclaimed John Leonard of the *New York Times* in discussing *One Hundred Years of Solitude*, "has been written by a Latin American."

GRANDFATHERS AND GHOSTS

A scene from village life in Colombia in the early 20th century. García Márquez grew up in Aracataca, a small rural town on Colombia's Caribbean coast. It is this world that is so often portrayed in his writing.

Gabriel José García Márquez was born on March 6, probably in the year 1928 but possibly a year earlier, in the village of Aracataca, Colombia. He was the first child born of the marriage between Luisa Santiaga Márquez Iguarán and Gabriel Eligio García. The writer usually cites 1928 as the year of his birth, but his father always insisted on the earlier date. It would be understandable if Gabriel Eligio García confused the birthdates of his children, for his marriage was to produce 11 more, and he had sired 4 others while still a bachelor. There was even another Gabriel among his progeny.

Gabito, as the firstborn was called—Gabito is a diminutive form of the name Gabriel; in adulthood the writer would be known to his friends and admirers as Gabo—was born in Aracataca as a gesture of reconciliation between his parents and maternal grandparents. His mother was one of two children born of the marriage between Colonel Nicolás Ricardo Márquez Mejía and Tranquilina Iguarán Cotes. The colonel, a hero of the defeated Liberal side in the War of a Thousand Days, was one of Aracataca's first citizens, and he and his wife strongly disapproved of

27

the attentions paid their daughter by Gabriel Eligio García, who wooed her obsessively with love letters, romantic poems, and violin serenades. The smitten suitor was illegitimate, for one thing; he had a reputation as a prodigious womanizer; he was a Conservative (the Liberals' opponents in the War of a Thousand Days and in the eternal struggle for political power in Colombia); and he was one of *la hojarasca*.

Literally, la hojarasca means dead or fallen leaves and, by extension, garbage or trash, something to be swept up and disposed of. It would be the name of García Márquez's first published work, a novella; and it was the name used by the longer established and resentful residents of Aracataca, such as his maternal grandparents, to refer to the newcomers who descended on their town during the heady boom days of the first decades of the 20th century, when the United Fruit Company, a U.S. conglomerate based in Boston, established itself there to make millions of dollars shipping bananas around the world.

The colonel and his wife discouraged the romance between their daughter and the bastard son of la hojarasca in every way they knew. They shipped

The house in Aracataca where García Márquez was born and in which he was raised by his grandparents. A return trip in later years inspired him to write the novella Leaf Storm: *"It was as if everything I saw had already been written, and all I had to do was sit down and copy what was already there and what I was just reading."*

Luisa off across the mountains to stay with relatives, and when she returned with her ardor undampened, the colonel used his considerable influence in Aracataca to have her suitor's employers transfer him to Riohacha, some hundred miles away to the northeast at the western edge of La Guajira, a desert peninsula. But Gabriel Eligio's trade enabled him to continue his pursuit of Luisa; a former medical student who had abandoned his studies because of a lack of funds, he earned his living as a telegraph operator and stubbornly tapped out messages of affection to his beloved over the wire, which were then relayed to her by a friend in the telegraph office in Aracataca. Such persistence rendered the colonel and his wife powerless, and they were forced to acquiesce in Luisa and Gabriel's marriage, though with one condition: The couple would live elsewhere than Aracataca. The newlyweds set up house in Riohacha, but when Luisa was nearing the time of the birth of her first son, her parents invited her to come home to deliver her baby. When Luisa returned to Riohacha several months later, she left the infant Gabito to be raised by her parents. The newlyweds were poor, and extended families are not unusual in the Caribbean. "It's a common story in the Caribbean," García Márquez said of how he came to be born and raised in Aracataca.

Aracataca's days as a boomtown came to an end the same year Gabriel García Márquez was born. Some 50 miles inland from the Caribbean Sea, on the Santa Marta railway line, the village lay in the heart of Colombia's banana zone. Though coffee has traditionally been Colombia's most important export, during the first three decades of the 20th century the banana crop was critical to the nation's economy and especially that of the Santa Marta district. At the time, Colombia was the world's leading producer of ba-

nanas, and the growth of the banana industry there
helped stimulate a period of unprecedented prosperity known as the "dance of the millions"; it also
engendered the social upheaval and turmoil of la
hojarasca.

The most important force in the Colombian banana industry, by far, was the United Fruit Company.
By the end of the 1920s, United Fruit controlled 60
percent of the banana trade worldwide and 75 percent
of the banana-producing land in the department of
Magdalena, of which Aracataca was a part. This near-
monopoly led to abusive practices: The company, for
example, routinely let 85 percent of the land it controlled in Colombia, all of which had been given to it
by the Colombian government, lie fallow in order to
manipulate banana prices on the world market. In a
poor country wracked by political violence, where,
then as now, land distribution was the single most
explosive political issue, such practices caused intense
resentment. The concessions granted the company by
the Colombian government, which was eager to en-
courage foreign investment, aroused further opposition: United Fruit was not obligated to pay export
taxes, and it exercised unlimited control over irriga-
tion waters within Magdalena. Other prerogatives it
simply seized: The company refused to allow independent banana producers to ship their fruit on the
Santa Marta railroad. Its Colombian employees were
paid only in company scrip, which could be redeemed
only in company stores as payment for the overpriced
goods with which the company ships filled their holds
so they would not have to return empty to Colombia
after delivering their cargo of bananas to the company
piers in New Orleans, Louisiana. Technically, however, the company had no employees; all its field hands,
who were paid piecework, were hired through sub-
contractors. This subterfuge enabled the company to

García Márquez's parents, Gabriel Eligio García and Luisa Márquez de García, photographed in the early 1980s. The couple's long and difficult courtship, which took place during the 1920s, would be retold by the author in his novel Love in the Time of Cholera.

avoid Colombian labor laws mandating such safeguards and necessities as lavatories, accident insurance, and hospital care; and enabled its lawyers to convince a Colombian court to rule that legally it had no workers. The company was so powerful within the banana district that it constituted a virtual state within a state.

On October 7, 1928, 32,000 field hands in Colombia's banana zone struck the United Fruit Company. Their demands included toilet facilities, basic health care, one day off a week, and payment in cash rather than scrip. The company refused to negotiate, and the Colombian government, then in the hands of the Conservative party, generally hostile to workers' interests, and fearful of U.S. intervention, sent troops to the department of Magdalena. The jailing of workers and the use of troops as scabs led to violent resistance by the strikers, and on December 5, the government officially declared the banana zone to be in a "state of siege."

That night, a huge crowd of workers gathered for a demonstration in the square near the railway station in the town of Ciénaga, some 30 miles north of Aracataca. General Cortés Vargas and his troops arrived at 1:30 on the morning of December 6 and commanded the crowd to disperse. When it did not, he ordered his troops to fire on the unarmed citizens. Casualty figures for the massacre range from 29 killed (the general's estimate) to "more than one thousand" dead (a U.S. diplomat) to 1,500 murdered (a Colombian labor union leader) to 3,000 slain (José Arcadio Segundo Buendía, in *One Hundred Years of Solitude*). Army trucks rumbled away into the night from the scene of the slaughter carrying corpses toward the sea; in the ensuing months of chaos, labor activists were rounded up by the army and "disappeared" into government custody, never to be seen again. On one rainy night, 120 strikers were executed in the Aracataca cemetery and were tumbled into a muddy common grave. The entire "incident" was downplayed, when mentioned at all, in the official press; a concerted effort was made by the government and its supporters to pretend that it had never happened. The standard secondary-school textbook on Colombian history that García Márquez would use as a student mentioned the strike but not the massacre: It said only that martial law had been declared and that after a time "tranquility" had been restored to the region. The future novelist would hear many of his fellow students and their parents insist that the mass execution had never happened; others would say that they had a relative or friend who died in the square that day.

Among those who would not be intimidated by the conspiracy of silence was the old Liberal war horse, Colonel Nicolás Márquez, García Márquez's grandfather. When, the year after the massacre, a young Liberal member of Congress, Jorge Eliécer Gaitán, convened hearings to inquire into the responsibility for the tragedy, Colonel Márquez gave testimony. Gaitán's fiery speech to Congress denouncing the murders was followed by "one of the most famous debates in Colombian parliamentary history," according to the Colombian historian Miguel Urrutia, and it made Gaitán the new hero of the Liberal party's radical wing.

His grandfather, García Márquez would say, was "the person I've gotten along with best and had the best communication with ever . . . the most important figure in my life." Disdainful of Conservatives, the banana fever, la hojarasca, and the gringos of the United Fruit Company, the gregarious old soldier told endless stories of his fighting in the service of the

Bananas being loaded onto railway cars by Central American workers. The oppressive policies of the United Fruit Company, a U.S. corporation, led to a strike of Colombian banana workers in 1928. The government's bloody repression of the strike was officially covered up, but García Márquez learned of it from his grandfather and later retold the story in One Hundred Years of Solitude.

Liberal cause during the War of a Thousand Days, and it was from him that his grandson received his first lessons in Colombian history.

Although Colombia prides itself on being one of the oldest functioning democracies in Latin America, the single most distinguishing facet of its history since its liberation from Spanish rule in 1819 has been its extraordinarily high level of political violence. Until the 1970s, this centered almost exclusively on the struggle for power between Colombia's two dominant political parties—the Liberals and the Conservatives.

The roots of the conflict between the Liberals and Conservatives, which made 19th-century Colombia a "country of permanent war," in the words of the historian Gonzalo Sánchez, date back to the early years of independence. Indeed, according to the political scientist David Bushnell, "In Colombia there was a national party politics even before there was truly speaking a national economy or a national culture." The division of the Colombian body politic along Liberal and Conservative lines arose initially out of ideological differences over the future course of the Colombian nation.

By the time Colombia's Rionegro Constitution was ratified in 1863, the ideological distinctions between the Liberals and Conservatives had been firmly established. The 1863 constitution was a quintessentially Liberal document in that it established a federal government—a sharing of power among Colombia's departments, or states—without a strong central authority. Under the Rionegro Constitution, for example, the central government could exercise political and military power only in foreign affairs. The Rionegro Constitution also prevented clergymen from holding public office; separated church and state; provided for mandatory secular education; eliminated qualifications based on income, property, and education from the right to vote; gave citizens the rights to own and traffic in firearms; and established direct elections for most local, state, and national offices—all positions that were staunchly opposed by the Conservatives. The great French novelist and poet of the time, Victor Hugo, an ardent republican, commented that the Rionegro Constitution was "written for a nation of angels." But as García Márquez's works would demonstrate, Colombia was inhabited by men, not angels, and too many issues divided the Liberals and the Conservatives for them to live in heavenly peace.

Ultimately, however, Liberals and Conservatives struggled less over ideology than over power. Though, since attaining its independence, Colombia has functioned (with brief interruptions) as a democracy, in the sense that regular elections are held, the party in power inevitably has maintained such a stranglehold over the machinery of government and the apparatus of elections that it is all but undefeatable. Between 1830 and 1958, the only (and rare) electoral changes of power that have occurred have been the result of the ruling party splitting into factions. During those years, a genuine electoral change of power occurred only once, in 1861. Invariably, elections have been characterized by a high degree of corruption on the part of the ruling power and by a large degree of cynicism, indifference, and lack of participation on the part of the electorate.

Once in power, the ruling party has been able to solidify its control in myriad ways, chiefly through its ability to make appointments at every level of government. According to the historian Paul Oquist, "The group that did not control the state could expect only discrimination from it, whereas those persons politically connected with the party in power could expect to monopolize state decision-making and the benefits to be derived from state power." The Conservative successor to the Rionegro Constitution, the Constitution of 1886, under which Colombia is still governed, gives the central government immense powers as far as the appointment of local and state officials. Under it, for example, the ruling party could appoint mayors (this power was delegated to municipalities in 1987), police chiefs, local judges, and even teachers in the public schools. "To lose power," according to a 1958 article in the Colombian magazine *Semana* (Week), "meant that the mayor of the town would turn into a dangerous enemy, that the official of the Agrarian Bank would refuse the loan, that the new teacher would look with disfavour on one's child attending school, that the official of the Department of Health would first attend his fellow partisan of the other party . . . and that it was necessary to keep a prudent distance from the local police."

Not surprisingly, those excluded from power often resorted to force of arms. During the 23 years of the

A depiction of the Battle of Carabobo (1821), an important event in Bolívar's liberation campaign. García Márquez's grandfather, Colonel Nicolás Márquez, told him many tales of the civil wars that followed Colombia's independence; the atmosphere of violence and oppression is a recurring feature in the novelist's work.

Rionegro Constitution, there were at least 40 rebellions and one civil war, the latter precipitated by the Liberals' attempt to institute secular education. After the Conservative accession to power in 1886 and the establishment of the new constitution, which reserved virtually all power to the central government, established a national army, and gave the Catholic church control over education and most civil ceremonies, the Liberals went into armed opposition in the form of guerrilla armies whose rank-and-file came from the poorest elements of Colombian society. In all, during the 19th century in Colombia, there were at least 70 armed rebellions, 14 local civil wars, 8 national civil wars, and 3 coups d'état.

This ceaseless bloodshed served to solidify party ties even as the ideological distinctions between the Liberals and Conservatives were blurring. (A sarcastic Colombian maxim defines the difference between the two as "the Liberals drink in public and pray in private, while Conservatives pray in public and drink in private," while a disillusioned Colonel Aureliano Buendía in *One Hundred Years of Solitude* puts it differently: "Conservatives go to mass at eleven, Liberals at five.") For the poorer members of Colombian society, who have always constituted the vast majority, the ideological differences between the two parties were never of great importance. Both parties were dominated by the elite elements of Colombian society, neither advocated radical reform, and no matter which party was in power, the poor suffered. They fought initially in defense of their own small plot of land or because a rich local landowner forced them to or offered them a reward for their service or because they were conscripted into the army, and they continued to fight because the other side had killed their father or cousin or son or friend or stolen their land. The violence thus gave birth to and nurtured implacable, long-lived hatreds that were eternally avenged and revenged; in the Colombian countryside, the political was made personal. A. E. Rothlisberger, a Swiss historian who wrote about the revolution of 1885, observed that "the majority do not fight in one party or another out of conviction but because they must avenge some atrocity"; a teen age Colombian participant in the War of a Thousand Days wrote that though the majority of men in the Liberal and Conservative armies had no clear idea why they were fighting, they killed each other nonetheless "with a dull, savage hatred."

Party membership in Colombia thus became as much a matter of family tradition, loyalty, and honor as one of ideology and power. It is no exaggeration to say that in Colombia one is born a Liberal or a Conservative. "Among the most remote childhood memories of a Colombian are . . . those of political parties similar to two races which live side by side but hate each other eternally," the scholar Hernández Rodríguez has written. "To change one's party loyalty," notes the historian Robert Dix, "is to be considered an apostate and a traitor. . . . Any change in political identification requires corresponding changes in one's closest social and personal relationships." This question of political affiliation affects virtually every element of day-to-day life in Colombia, as García Márquez would examine in *No One Writes to the Colonel*, *In Evil Hour*, and *One Hundred Years of Solitude*.

The 19th-century struggle for power in Colombia reached its awful culmination in the War of a Thousand Days, which at that time was by far Colombia's most devastating civil conflict. The war began in October 1899; General Rafael Uribe Uribe, the legendary leader of the Liberals whose career helped inspire the character of Colonel Aureliano Buendía, finally laid down his arms on October 24, 1902, at a banana plantation named Neerlandia, not far from Aracataca. By that time, according to the Colombian politician Jorge Holguin, it was as if "a gust of death had passed over the country"; more than 100,000 Colombians had died, most of them peasants, many of them boys in their teens. One consequence of the subsequent exhaustion was a cessation, for several decades, of political warfare in Colombia; another was Colombia's helplessness in the face of the secession—engineered by the United States, which wished to build a canal there—of the departments that would soon become the free nation of Panama.

For men like Colonel Nicolás Márquez, the wars between the Liberals and the Conservatives were the outstanding events of their youth, and young García

Workers construct the massive Gatun Locks of the Panama Canal during the early 1900s. In order to gain permission to build the canal, the United States engineered the secession of several of Colombia's departments, which then joined to form the new nation of Panama.

Márquez could not help but be impressed by the tales of those days told by his grandfather. Scented, dressed always in a vest and tie, with a pocket watch and a gold chain, the colonel was the patriarch of his sprawling house in Aracataca. From him, García Márquez learned not only history but of the power of nostalgia. "When he spoke of the civil wars," his grandson would recall, "he spoke of them as almost pleasant experiences—sort of youthful adventures with guns. Nothing like the wars of today. Oh, certainly, the civil wars had many terrible battles and many, many deaths. But during that time, my grandfather also had a great many love affairs and he also fathered a great many children."

Those children—so many of them that their exact number was never known, though 16 was the number most often used—wandered in and out of the colonel's household; throughout his lifetime, García Márquez would constantly be meeting new aunts and uncles. Tranquilina, the colonel's wife and cousin, was a "very, very jealous woman. But when she'd hear of one those children's being born, she reacted like Ursula Buendía: She took it into her household. My grandmother said that the family blood couldn't just wander around out there, lost. Anyway, she loved those children a lot. There was a point in that house when you couldn't tell which children came from the marriage and which didn't."

There were many other things about his grandfather that made a great impression on the young grandson with the imagination and soul of a future novelist. In his youth, in his hometown of Riohacha, the colonel had shot and killed another man in a duel, and for the rest of his days he bore the guilt of that act as if it were a scar. "You can't believe how a dead man weighs you down," he often said, and it was following the duel that he moved to Aracataca. With unexpectant anticipation he awaited the arrival of the pension check that the government had promised the veterans of the War of a Thousand Days as a gesture of reconciliation. It never arrived, and after his death Tranquilina waited some more. Each year, the colonel took Gabito to see the circus when it came to Aracataca and then gave him zoology lessons from the dictionary about dromedaries and other exotic creatures. And the writer never forgot that distant afternoon when his grandfather took him to the company stores of the United Fruit Company to discover ice.

"Throughout my adult life, whenever something happens to me, above all whenever something good comes my way, I feel that the only thing I need in order for my happiness to be complete, is that my grandfather should know about it," García Márquez has said on more than one occasion. Aspects of his grandfather's character and experience inform several of the writer's literary creations.

The writer's grandmother, Tranquilina Iguarán de Márquez, was a more frightening figure than her husband, but she exerted no less an influence on little Gabito. She and her sisters, several of whom resided in the colonel's house at various times, lived in a world of portents and signs, where the boundary between the land of the living and the land of the dead was easily crossed. She was a living repository of the folklore that characterized the culture of the Caribbean coast of Colombia at the time, and her admonitions and maxims were uttered in a matter-of-fact tone that implied there could be no questioning the truth of what she said. Though she took loving care of young Gabito, much of what she said scared him, even though his grandfather cautioned him to disregard most of her statements as impractical. "Don't listen to that," he would say. "Those are women's beliefs." His grandmother's words stayed with him nonetheless.

"My grandfather's house was a house of many women—my grandmother, my grandmother's sister, others," García Márquez remembered in 1983:

> My grandfather and I were the only two males there. The women were incredibly superstitious, crazy—crazy in the sense that they were people with imagination. . . . With my grandmother, every natural event had a supernatural interpretation. If a butterfly flew in the window, she'd declare, 'A letter is coming today.' If milk boiled over on the stove, she'd say, 'We must be careful—someone in the family is sick.' When I was a child, my grandmother would wake me in the night and tell me horrible stories of people who, for some reason, had a presentiment of their death, of the dead who appeared, of the dead who didn't appear. Often, our house in Aracataca, our huge house, seemed as if it were haunted.

One of those who had a presentiment of their own death was García Márquez's Aunt Francisca. An adept in the supernatural who was often consulted by the townspeople to interpret omens, Aunt Francisca, though in the best of health, one day began knitting a burial shroud, which she announced was to be her own. When questioned why by little Gabito, she responded, "Because I'm going to die, little boy." When the shroud was finished, she took to her bed, never to rise again. (Amaranta Buendía, in *One Hundred Years of Solitude*, knits her own burial shroud and then dies.) Two of the dead who did not appear, much to Gabito's relief, were also members of the household:

> In that house there was an empty room where Aunt Petra had died. There was an empty room where Uncle Lazarus had died. And so, at night, you couldn't walk in that house, because the dead outnumbered the living. They would sit me down, at six in the evening, in a corner, and they would say to me: "Don't move from there, be-

cause, if you do, Aunt Petra, who is in her room, will come, or Uncle Lazarus."

"I always stayed sitting," García Márquez remembered. "In my first novel, *Leaf Storm*, one of the characters is a boy of seven, who through all the novel, is sitting in a small chair. Now I realize that there is something of me in that boy, sitting in that small chair, in a house full of fears."

Through his first eight years, until the death of his grandfather and the blindness of his grandmother, García Márquez had little contact with his parents, aside from regular visits that grew more frequent once they moved back to Aracataca. His earliest memory of his mother is of a day when he was awakened early and told to put on his best clothes because she was coming to visit:

> I remember going into a room, and there were very many women sitting there, and I felt disconcerted, because I didn't know which one was my mother. . . . Then she embraced me and I became very frightened, because I felt I didn't love her. I'd heard one was supposed to love one's parents very much, and it seemed evil that I didn't.

Despite these beginnings, García Márquez regards his relationship with his mother as "perhaps the most serious relationship I have had in my life." In his novella *Crónica de una muerte anunciada* (Chronicle of a Death Foretold), which was published in 1982, she appears, with her own name, Luisa Santiaga, as the mother of the narrator and is portrayed, like most of the writer's female characters, as resolute and indomitable within the sphere of her household domain. Moreover, "in spite of the fact that she hadn't gone out into the streets in years, not even to attend mass," she is the only character who acts—albeit, through no fault of her own, too late—to prevent the gruesome and senseless murder that is the subject of the story. In

The main square of Bogotá, Colombia's capital and largest city, as it appeared to an artist in 1837. Bogotá's inhabitants considered themselves more refined than the costeños—the Colombians living along the country's Caribbean coast—and for this reason García Márquez, who considered himself a costeño, always disliked the capital.

so doing, she allows her individual conscience to override familial allegiances, an anachronistic sense of honor, and an outmoded view of male-female relations; "for once in her life she didn't even pay any attention to her husband" because "you always have to take the side of the dead."

In another place in the same story, García Márquez portrays his mother as the possessor of secret knowledge, and one senses that the relationship between them was a tender and affectionate one:

> It was even stranger that my mother didn't know either, because she knew about everything before anyone else in the house, in spite of the fact that she hadn't gone out into the street in years, not even to attend mass. I had become aware of that quality of hers ever since I began to get up early for school. I would find her the way she was in those days, pale and stealthy, sweeping the courtyard with a homemade broom in the ashen glow of dawn, and between sips of coffee she would proceed to tell me what had happened in the world while we'd been asleep. She seemed to have secret threads of communication with the

other people in town, especially those her age, and sometimes she would surprise us with news so ahead of its time that she could only have known it through powers of divination.

The writer's relationship with his father, Gabriel Eligio García, was much less profound; he has commented often that he never really knew his father. Nevertheless, there were aspects of his father's character and experience that greatly influenced him, most notably the family legend of Gabriel Eligio's relentless courtship, against the opposition of the colonel and his wife, of Luisa Santiaga. That romance inspired García Márquez's novel of undying devotion, *El amor en los tiempos del cólera* (Love in the Time of Cholera), in which the youthful courtship of the haughty beauty Fermina Daza by the lovelorn swain Florentino Ariza, with his violin serenades and impassioned telegraphic communications, recapitulates in "rigorously historical" form his parents' romance.

Though García Márquez remembers his hometown with less fondness than he does his family, its influence on his writing has been no less great. "I think of [Aracataca] as a horrible boom town," he said in 1983. "It was a banana center for the United Fruit Company—a place where people came to enrich themselves as quickly as possible." He recalls it as an unpaved village of "wooden shacks with roofs made of zinc and tin," except for the section claimed by the United Fruit Company, where its North American employees lived in huge houses with swimming pools and manicured lawns, guarded by barbed-wire fences and attack dogs.

Yet there were aspects of Aracataca and the surrounding regions that the young boy (and the mature writer) took great delight in. Colombia is a huge country, unique among the nations of South America in that it has coastlines on both the Pacific Ocean and the Caribbean Sea. Its great size and the ruggedness of much of its terrain—the country is dominated by the three ranges of the Andes Mountains: the Cordillera Oriental, the Cordillera Central, and the Cordillera Occidental—made transportation and communication difficult until the 20th century and ensured that many of the regions developed in isolation from one another. The result has been regional differences in culture and population so distinct that it is often said that Colombia is a "kind of archipelago" rather than a nation.

García Márquez comes from the northern, Caribbean coastal region of Colombia. This tropical region was the first explored and settled by the Spanish conquistadores in the 16th century—Columbus, on his last voyage, "discovered" the Magdalena River; Santa Marta was the first Spanish settlement in Colombia, and Cartagena is the nation's oldest continuously inhabited Spanish city—but for several centuries now the vast majority of Colombia's population has lived in the cool mountain highlands or in the valleys of the Cauca and Magdalena rivers, which divide the cordilleras. There is a great rivalry between the two regions, and the denizens of one often regard the inhabitants of the other with condescension if not outright disdain. To the *costeños* (coastals) of the Caribbean, the *cachacos*—an untranslatable nickname, often pejorative, used by the people of the coast to refer to the highland dwellers—tend to be uncomfortably stiff, formal, haughty, and aristocratic. As Bogotá, the nation's capital, is 9,000 feet up in the Cordillera Oriental, the culture of the mountains is also associated with the central government, which in a Liberal bastion like Aracataca has long been seen as an oppressive force. Bogotá was also the capital of the Spanish colony of Nueva Granada, and among its upper classes a pride in one's European roots—and white skin—still prevails to an extent unknown in the Caribbean.

The Caribbean coast has a much different feel to it. The climate, as opposed to Bogotá's year-round 58 degrees, is tropical, with intense heat and a rainy season, called winter, that lasts from late April to early December. Male costeños are more likely to wear loose-fitting, embroidered *guayabera* shirts than coats and ties, and the Spanish spoken there is notable for the spontaneous flair of its slang, as opposed to the elegant formality of the language as spoken in Bogotá, whose residents pride themselves on speaking the best Spanish in the world. Most costeños, including García Márquez and his family, are mestizos (literally, mixed),

Simón Bolívar (1783–1830), known as the Liberator, led popular revolts against Spanish rule in Latin America during the early 19th century and served as Colombia's first president. Steeped in the lore of Colombia's past since childhood, García Márquez portrayed Bolívar in his 1990 novel, The General in His Labyrinth.

meaning that their ancestry is a combination of Spanish, Indian, and, in some cases, African roots. The port city of Cartagena, on the coast west of Aracataca, was a center of the Spanish trade in African slaves; 30 miles south of Cartagena is the legendary region of Palenque, founded by runaway slaves in 1599. African place names are common in northern Colombia; Macondo is, in fact, a Bantu word that means "banana." Much of the popular music of the coast has its roots in African forms. The region is also rich in the kind of folk beliefs passed on to young Gabito by his grandmother; Aracataca is especially famous for belief in such tales.

García Márquez has always considered himself a costeño and a mestizo. "Where I really feel at home is the Caribbean," he has said, and he regards his costeño identity as crucial to his work: "Because I'm Caribbean, recognizing this fact made me see into myself and realize I'm a *mestizo* and at the same time made me start observing more clearly the historical conditions of our countries." All of his novels and novellas are set in the Caribbean region he knew as a young boy, with its drenching rains and enervating heat, and in several he draws on specific episodes of the region's rich history—the English buccaneer Sir Francis Drake's sacking of Riohacha in 1595 figures in *One Hundred Years of Solitude* as the indirect, humorous "cause" of the founding of Macondo; the massacre of the striking banana workers at Ciénaga is a crucial episode in the same novel; and the last voyage of the liberator of Latin America from Spanish rule, Simón Bolívar, which ended at Santa Marta, forms the subject of his most recent novel, *El general en su laberinto* (The General in His Labyrinth).

Indeed, the coastal region where García Márquez spent the first eight years of his life in the house of his grandfather has been the single greatest influence on his work as a writer, shaping his frames of reference, providing him with a sense of history, exciting his imagination, and giving him his language. "Clearly, the Latin American environment is marvelous," he said in 1983:

> Particularly the Caribbean. I happen to come from the Caribbean part of Colombia, which is a fantastic place—completely different from the Andean part, the highlands. During the colonial part of Colombian history, all the people who considered themselves respectable went to the interior—to Bogotá. On the coast, all that were left were bandits—bandits in the good sense— and dancers, adventurers, people full of gaiety. The costeños were descendants of pirates and smugglers, with a mixture of black slaves. To grow up in such an environment is to have fantastic resources for poetry. Also, in the Caribbean we are capable of believing anything, because we have the influences of all those different cultures, mixed in with Catholicism and our own local beliefs. I think that gives us an open-mindedness to look beyond apparent reality.

When Gabito was eight, his grandfather died, and he went to live with his parents, who were then residing in the river port of Sucre, far to the southwest of Aracataca. "Nothing interesting has happened to me since," he has said on many occasions. "I feel that all my writing has been about the experiences of the time I spent with my grandparents. . . . From that period of my life, and from my life in general, what remain for me are flashes of memory that I hardly analyze. I prefer only the sensations they leave."

A view of Bogotá's Avenida Quesada in the 1940s. Poor and depressed during his student days in the capital, García Márquez rode the trolley cars from morning to night, reading poetry. He found the city's perpetual autumnal rain especially dismal, later describing it as a "centuries-old drizzle."

THE OLD MAN'S
APPRENTICESHIP

García Márquez has consistently maintained that his parents' decision to let the colonel and his wife raise him did not leave him with a feeling of abandonment. "I just thought life was like that," he has said. "Perhaps, in another kind of society, I might have felt abandoned. But in the Caribbean, it's perfectly natural to live with grandparents and aunts and uncles." Likewise, he has said that the death of his grandfather was not a devastating experience for him. "I practically didn't realize it. Besides, as an eight-year-old, I didn't have any clear notion what death meant. Having a Catholic upbringing, I probably thought he'd gone to heaven and was very content." Still, one senses the confusion and loneliness he must have known as a little boy in the answer he unfailingly gives when asked why he writes: "I write so that my friends will love me more. I have always said that. I don't seek admiration. Or recognition. Or glory. I want them to love me. That's the truth. That's sincere. But it's also very sad. . . . My great problem is to be loved more, and that is why I write."

With the death of his grandfather, Gabito left Aracataca to join his parents and sisters and brothers in

Sucre, where his father had taken a job as a pharmacist, but he did not spend a great deal of time in the family household. He was sent almost immediately to a boarding school, the Colegio San José, in Barranquilla, a cosmopolitan Caribbean port city at the mouth of the Magdalena River. There, though he was quiet and profoundly shy—a trait that persists: he claims today, despite his fame, to "be the shyest man in the world. . . . On this I accept no argument or debate"—he won popularity with his teachers and fellow students for his skill in composing humorous poems, a facility he demonstrated anew at the Colegio de Jesuitas, also in Barranquilla, where he transferred when he was about 10. He also drew cartoons, a pastime he had begun at home before he could even read or write and that he regards as the true beginning of his literary career. Gabito was a thin, silent, solitary boy who rarely participated in sports or school-yard games, so serious that his classmates called him the Old Man.

In 1940, Gabito won a scholarship to the Liceo Nacional, a secondary school for Colombia's most gifted students located in Zipaquirá, a city in the Andes some 30 miles north of Bogotá. To get there, he had to make a riverboat voyage up the Magdalena and then take a train high into the mountains to the capital and on to Zipaquirá; the entire journey took a week. His first experience of the cachaco world of the highlands indelibly impressed upon him that he was a child of the Caribbean, a costeño through and through. Bogotá's perpetual autumnal rain—a "centuries-old drizzle" he calls it in *The General in His Labyrinth*—chilled his bones and saddened his soul; he wept when he stepped off his train and many times afterward.

"Of all the cities I know," he said many years later, "none has made such an impression on me as Bogotá. I arrived from Barranquilla . . . at five o'clock in the afternoon . . . and that was the most dismal experience in the whole of my youth. Bogotá was dismal, smelling of soot, and the drizzle fell unceasingly, and men dressed in black, with black hats, went stumbling through the streets. . . . You only saw a woman occasionally, since they were not allowed in the majority of public places." His feelings about the Colombian capital never really changed. Though Bogotá would always be for García Márquez, as for all costeño Liberals, "that remote and unreal city" that "was the center of gravity of the power which had been imposed upon us since our earliest times," his dislike was cultural as well as political. "There are cities with ships and cities without ships. That is the only acceptable distinction, the only true essential difference," the proud young costeño would write in his first days as a journalist.

His feelings for neighboring Zipaquirá differed little from those he held toward Bogotá, but he found much to stimulate his intelligence and imagination at school. Though Gabito was strongest in the humanities—Spanish, literature, and history—he learned much from his mathematics and science instructors. Some of his teachers in those subjects were socialists, and at recesses or after school they would discuss economic and political theory with Gabito, who was

A settlement along Colombia's Magdalena River. To reach Bogotá from Aracataca, García Márquez had to make a riverboat voyage up the Magdalena and then continue on by train high into the mountains. The entire journey took a week.

fascinated by their analyses of the inequities in Colombian and Latin American society.

But it was literature that was always his first inspiration. In the school dormitories at night, the students
often entertained themselves by reading novels aloud,
and it was Gabito to whom they most often turned to
make the evening's selection. Among the novels he
remembers himself and his fellows reading in such
fashion are *The Three Musketeers*, by Alexandre Dumas;
Twenty Thousand Leagues Under the Sea, by Jules Verne;
and *The Magic Mountain*, by Thomas Mann. The first
two are romantic adventure stories—a swashbuckler
and science fiction, respectively—that have long been
popular with young male readers, but the third is a
lengthy, enormously complex novel of ideas that is
usually regarded as one of the greatest literary works
of the 20th century. It is a measure of García Márquez's literary sophistication at a young age that he
would select such a title for the enjoyment of himself
and his fellows. The mixture of literary complexity
with the most time-honored elements of popular
storytelling, as represented in the selection of titles, is
also telling and would come to be characteristic of his
own fiction. It is significant as well that none of these
novels was written by a Latin American or Spanish
writer. Part of Latin America's solitude, as García
Márquez would come to see it, was that its writers had
not yet done justice to its experience, and his greatest
literary influences would all be from elsewhere.

Gabito's literary taste was enough to convince his
fellow students that he had a vocation, though it was
as yet apparent to himself only as a matter of predilec-
tion, not achievement. "The funny thing," he remembered in 1981, "is that I now realize that when I was
in high school I had the reputation of being a writer
though I never in fact wrote anything." Though it is
clear that by the time he graduated from the Liceo
Nacional in 1946 he also considered himself a

writer—becoming a journalist and writing novels were two of the goals he set for himself—this was still a matter more of image than reality, for instead of beginning a literary career he bowed to his parents' wishes and enrolled as a law student at the Universidad Nacional in Bogotá.

Before starting at the university in February 1947, he spent some months with his family in Sucre, where he had also been spending his vacations from school over the past several years. There, he learned lessons about the power and the horror of love. On one of his visits, he met and was enchanted by Mercedes Barcha Pardo, a dark-eyed, silent, schoolgirl beauty of Egyptian descent whom he would nickname the "sacred crocodile" and always regard as the most interesting person he has ever met. During his stay at home after his graduation from the Liceo Nacional, he proposed marriage to her. He was 18; she was 13, according to some accounts, or possibly even younger; to this day the writer professes not to know her exact age. "Many knew that in the confusion of the bash I had proposed marriage to Mercedes Barcha as soon as she finished primary school, just as she herself would remind me fourteen years later when we got married," García Márquez would write in *Chronicle of a Death Foretold*, his novella about a less well destined courtship that took place in Sucre at about the same general time: Cayetano Gentile, a friend of the author's and of his family, was slaughtered by the brothers of Margarita Chica on being named as her seducer, after her newlywed husband returned her in shame to her family on their wedding night upon discovering that she was not a virgin. Sucre would also serve as the inspiration for the unnamed village—a "village in which there is no magic," according to García Márquez—that is the setting for *No One Writes to the Colonel*, *In Evil Hour*, and some of the short stories that were collected in *Los Funerales de la Mama Grande* (Big Mama's Funeral).

An illustration from Jules Verne's Twenty Thousand Leagues Under the Sea, *one of the novels García Márquez and his fellow students read aloud in their dormitory at the Liceo Nacional. As a student, García Márquez already had a literary reputation, although, as he readily admitted, "I never in fact wrote anything."*

Once back in Bogotá, the aspiring writer found that the study of the law was not for him, and he was heartsick once again. Depressed and lonesome, he neglected himself and his studies, and skipped classes and his morning shave in favor of endless rides on trolley cars—a cheap pleasure for a near-penniless student—made with no fixed destination in mind and a book of poetry his only company. Home was a boardinghouse; most of his meals were taken in cheap cafés. Despite the loneliness and desolation, he made several important friends at the university. Among these was Plinio Apuleyo Mendoza, who shared García Márquez's interest in journalism, and the well-born Camilo Torres, who would win fame (infamy, in some circles) as a rebel priest, one of the first practitioners of liberation theology in Latin America.

He made literary discoveries as well. One day a friend gave him, in Spanish translation by the great Argentine writer Jorge Luis Borges, a copy of the famous story *The Metamorphosis*, by the Austrian writer Franz Kafka, which had first been published in 1915. The story begins with the deathless line, "As

Gregor Samsa awoke one morning from uneasy dreams he found himself transformed in bed into a gigantic insect" and goes on to relate the ill-fated commercial traveler's doomed efforts to adapt to his predicament. Though fantastic, Samsa's situation is never treated as such by the author, whose attention remains focused on the myriad details and difficulties that would logically proceed from such a metamorphosis. No attempt is made to explain how or why the unfortunate Samsa was transformed; the metamorphosis is simply a given, stated matter-of-factly in the first line. The reader is convinced of the "reality" of the transformation through Kafka's success in portraying—from the point of view of Samsa—the situations and feelings that would inevitably result from such an unlikely event, none of which are themselves fantastic: the salesman has to eat new foods, learn how to move about in his new body, suffers unbearable loneliness when his family quite naturally is horrified by his new being. This attention to detail is evident from the opening, when Samsa "lying on his hard, as it were armor-plated, back" lifts "his head a little" to "see his dome-like brown belly divided into stiff arched segments on top of which the bed quilt could hardly keep in position and was about to slide off completely. His enormous legs, which were pitifully thin compared to the rest of his bulk, waved helplessly before his eyes." Through Kafka's depiction of such details, the story maintains a meticulous internal logic and attains its masterfully unnerving tone.

The Metamorphosis affected García Márquez like nothing he had ever read before. "The first line almost knocked me off the bed. I was so surprised," he later remembered. "When I read the line I thought to myself that I didn't know anyone was allowed to write things like that. If I had known, I would have started writing a long time ago." In Kafka's matter-of-fact relation of the fantastic, García Márquez heard the echoes of his grandmother's voice: "That's how my grandma used to tell stories, the wildest things with a completely natural tone of voice," he said about Kafka. "I now understood that there existed other possibilities in literature besides the rational and academic ones I'd learned about in secondary school. And I found my true path as a writer."

The adrift student now had a focus. Though García Márquez had entered the university proud, in his own words, that "I had a very good literary background in general, considerably above the average of my friends," he now recognized that he had a tremendous amount to learn if he wanted to write. Disdainful, then as now, of literary criticism and theorizing, he knew nonetheless that a career as a writer required a great deal of preparation, and he set himself a rigorous course of study—nothing less than a self-taught tutorial in the history of fiction. "Literature is a science one has to learn," he said many years later, when he was entitled to speak as a master, "and there are 10,000 years standing behind every short story that gets written. And to know literature you need modesty and humility. All the modesty that gets in the way of writing is needed in order to study all of literature, to know what the hell was being done 10,000 years ago, where we stand in the history of mankind. . . . Ultimately you learn literature not in the university but from reading and rereading other writers."

He began his study first thing the morning after reading *The Metamorphosis*. "I set out just like that, at eight o'clock next morning, to find out what the hell had been done in the novel from the Bible on up to what was being written at the time. For the next six years I dropped out of studying, dropped out of everything," he remembered.

And he began writing. In 1947, Eduardo Zalamea Borda, literary editor of the Bogotá newspaper *El*

Austrian author Franz Kafka (1883–1924), whose story The Metamorphosis, *the tale of a young man who is transformed into a giant insect, had a profound effect on the young García Márquez: "The first line almost knocked me off the bed," he later recalled.*

Espectador (The Spectator), published an essay in which he lamented the apparent dearth of talent among the current generation of Colombian writers. In response, García Márquez wrote and submitted for Zalamea Borda's consideration "The Third Resignation," a short story about a young man of 25 buried in a coffin, apparently dead for 18 years, yet who continues to have thoughts and sensations and even to grow. The Sunday after it was submitted, García Márquez was stunned to find his story published in *El Espectador*'s literary supplement, with an introduction by Zalamea Borda describing the young author as "the new genius of Colombian letters."

Overwhelmed by the older man's generous praise, the young writer felt as if it conferred on him a great responsibility, one for which in later years he was to feel that he had not been quite ready. Ten more of his short stories were to appear in *El Espectador* over the next five or six years; collected later and published as *Los ojos de un perro azul* (Eyes of a Blue Dog), these were the stories that the mature García Márquez would dismiss as "simply intellectual elaborations, nothing to do with my reality." The problem with the *El Espectador* stories, García Márquez would come to see, with their themes of isolation, alienation, and death and emphasis on nightmarish or surreal states of consciousness, is that they were products solely of his intellectual rather than his actual experience. Despite their success, he was never entirely happy with them. As a writer, he was still feeling his way; he had "not yet found the link between literature and real life," nor the theme that would allow him to use his own experience as illumination, nor the language—the voice—with which to express his inspiration. His search for these necessary elements of great fiction would take "the new genius of Colombian letters" almost 20 more years.

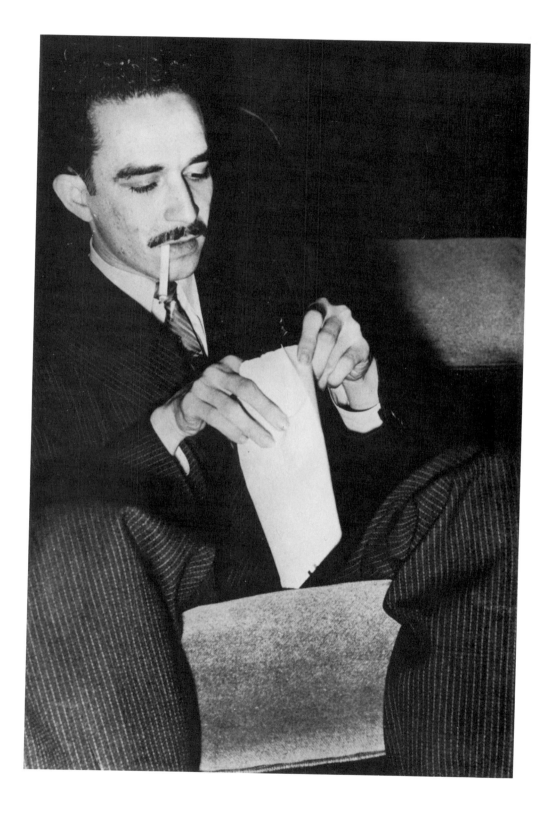

LA VIOLENCIA

At five minutes after one o'clock on the afternoon of April 9, 1948, on a crowded street in downtown Bogotá, Jorge Eliécer Gaitán, leader of the Liberal party and voice of Colombia's poor, was gunned down by a lone assassin who claimed to be the pawn of "powerful forces." The gunman was quickly stomped to death and dragged through the streets by an irate mob whose numbers grew to incredible proportions as news of the assassination spread. Rioters took control of Bogotá's streets, looting liquor stores and churches and sacking government buildings, including the Capitol. The offices of the Conservative daily newspaper *El Siglo* (The Century) were burned to the ground. Trolleys and cars were overturned and set ablaze. When *el bogotazo* (roughly, "the Bogotá coup") finally exhausted itself after three days and nights of violence, an estimated 2,500 people lay dead in the streets, and the capital was in ruins.

Since the time of the banana massacre in Ciénaga, Gaitán had been the champion of Colombia's peasants and working class. He was hated and feared by the elite elements of both major political parties, who contemptuously and fearfully nicknamed him "the Wolf" and "the Idiot." Although he was neither a Communist nor a radical, the threatened elements in

García Márquez early in his career as a journalist. When the University of Bogotá was closed, García Márquez took a job with El Universal in Cartagena. His work for the paper soon gained him widespread notice.

both parties labeled him as such. He believed in capitalism, albeit in a "socially responsible" form, and was a staunch advocate of Colombia's constitutional form of democracy. What Gaitán did wish to do was to close the gap between the "formal" Colombia of constitutions and democracy and the "real" Colombia in which the majority of its citizens had no effective say in government and the entrenched interests of both parties constituted a virtual oligarchy. Using the new technology of radio, he broadcast his message throughout the country. That message, according to historian Jenny Pearce, was simple: "While a bipartisan oligarchy monopolised wealth and political power, the mass of the people lived in poverty." Gaitán, according to Pearce, "spoke clearly of uniting the 'people' against the 'oligarchy,' the 'real' country against the 'political' country." "What is the difference between liberal hunger and conservative hunger?" Gaitán asked. "Malaria is neither conservative nor liberal." Nearly 30 years after el bogotazo, García Márquez observed that "the only new thing that Gaitán had to say was a very old truth that nobody dared to speak: 'The Liberal peasant and the Conservative peasant are exploited equally by the Liberal oligarchy and the Conservative oligarchy.'"

Initially, Gaitán's rise posed the greatest threat to the Liberals, his own party, who had taken power in 1930 after 45 years of Conservative rule when the Conservatives, riven by faction, split their ticket among two candidates for president. Gaitán's ascension resulted in a similar split among the Liberals in 1946 between himself and Gabriel Turbay, an old-style aristocratic oligarch who was rumored to be the lover of the *norteamericana* film star Joan Crawford. The Conservatives were returned to power, and the bloodiest period in Colombia's long history of civil strife, *la violencia* (the violence), began.

Fearful of *gaitanismo*, the Conservatives organized paramilitary forces in the countryside for the purpose of intimidating potential Liberal voters and running them off their land. Strikes and demonstrations by opponents of the government occurred frequently, and in 1947 the Liberals won control of the Congress, with Gaitán recognized as the undisputed party leader. His galvanizing effect on Colombian politics is indicated by the voter-turnout figures for the 1947 Congressional elections: 63.7 percent of the eligible electorate cast a ballot, despite the violence in the countryside and villages (which by the end of the year had claimed the lives of 14,000 victims), as opposed to just 39.4 percent two years earlier. On February 7, 1948, Gaitán led a silent march of 100,000 demonstrators through the streets of Bogotá to protest the ongoing violence. "All we ask, Mr. President," he said

Jorge Eliécer Gaitán, leader of Colombia's Liberal party. Colombia's poor felt that Gaitán was their only true voice in Colombian politics. His assassination on April 9, 1948, set off el bogotazo, *a three-day riot.*

in the speech he delivered that day, "is guarantees for human life, which is all that a nation can ask." A little more than two months later, he was assassinated, and la violencia entered its most brutal phase.

Between 1948 and 1953, 150,000 Colombians were killed as a result of la violencia. Rich Conservatives hired armies of gunmen, and the government used the police and paramilitary organizations to enforce its will; in response Liberal landowners and peasants organized guerrilla armies. As the killing escalated, la violencia generated its own momentum. Atrocity was avenged by atrocity. Villages were burned, families massacred, men castrated and flayed alive, women raped, babies spitted on bayonets. Terror became a conscious tactic; new and ever more gruesome methods of torture and murder were invented. Bloodshed, terror, and the amassing of wealth went hand-in-hand. "Anyone who had the guns and the power could and would steal away other people's property," wrote Gene Bell-Villada, author of the best work in English on García Márquez. Nearly 400,000 farms were seized in this manner, and at least 2 million peasants abandoned their land for the cities or emigrated to Venezuela. The violence reached from the countryside into the very halls of Congress, where in September 1949 Conservative members drew pistols and opened fire on a Liberal speaker, shooting him dead. The Conservative president, Mariano Ospina Pérez, responded by dissolving Congress, removing Liberals from all government positions, and declaring an official state of siege, which remained in effect until 1979. Governmental repression of the Liberals intensified, resulting in a state of permanent rebellion in much of the countryside. The rebels were classified by the government as "bandits" and "Communists," though in fact very few of them were committed political ideologues of any type. Colombia descended into a state of virtual barbarism.

El bogotazo and la violencia forced García Márquez to rethink his attitude toward fiction. Already, his reading of such North American writers as William Faulkner and Ernest Hemingway had made him realize that "their literature had a relationship with life that my short stories didn't." Then, el bogotazo, when "the people of Bogotá went raving mad in the streets," made him, he later said, "aware of the kind of country I was living in, and how little my short stories had to do with any of that. When I was later forced to go back to Barranquilla, on the Caribbean, where I had spent my childhood, I realized that that was the type of life I had lived, knew, and wanted to write about." García Márquez joined in the looting and rioting, but was himself greatly upset when he returned to his boardinghouse and found it aflame, his manuscripts and books still inside.

One immediate result of el bogotazo was the closing of the Universidad Nacional, for which García Márquez was not ungrateful. He returned to the north, which was much less affected by the violence, as a transfer student at the Universidad de Cartagena, but his matriculation there was little more than a formality to satisfy his parents: he rarely attended class and never graduated. Instead, he began his career as a journalist. Despite his dissatisfaction with them, the *El Espectador* stories had attracted some favorable notice—"probably because no one in Colombia was writing intellectual short stories," he joked later—and he was asked by the editors of *El Universal*, a new Cartagena daily newspaper, to write a 500-word daily column, which soon proved a popular feature.

After work at the newspaper, he continued his literary education. He had become friendly with some costeño literati—Germán Vargas, a literary critic; Alfonso Fuenmayor, a journalist; Álvaro Cepeda Samudio, a fellow aspiring novelist, and Ramón Vinyes, a Catalan bookseller and unpublished playwright and

Downtown Bogotá after el bogotazo, which left 2,500 people dead. García Márquez took part in the rioting and was also its victim: some of his manuscripts and beloved books were lost in a fire when the building he lived in burned.

novelist—who would become famous as the Barranquilla Group. It was these friends whom García Márquez wrote in as characters to the final two chapters of *One Hundred Years of Solitude*. Whenever he had some free time, García Márquez took the bus from Cartagena to Barranquilla to spend endless hours with these new friends in the Japi Bar, talking about literature and life. When he fell ill in late 1949 with pneumonia and had to return to his parents' house in Sucre for several months, these good fellows responded to his desperate plea for reading material by shipping him three wooden crates filled with Spanish translations of works by Faulkner, Hemingway, James Joyce, Virginia Woolf, and others.

Another literarily inclined friend, a law student named Gustavo Ibarra, with whom García Márquez spent much time in Cartagena's taverns, warned him that his study of fiction was focusing too much on the modern. "All these things you're reading are well and good," he told the aspiring novelist, "but they lack a base. You need a foundation." At Ibarra's suggestion, García Márquez began reading the plays of Sophocles, the 5th-century B.C. Greek dramatist whose works constitute the basis of the Western tradition of literary tragedy.

Of the plays of Sophocles, García Márquez was most influenced by *Oedipus Rex*, in which the protagonist, the king of Thebes, tragically fulfills the terrible fate foretold for him—that he would kill his father and marry his mother, and by *Antigone*, whose protagonist defies the laws of the community to bury her brother.

More than any other work, García Márquez would say, *Oedipus Rex* taught him about the pitfalls of power—a natural subject of interest for a politically aware, aspiring Latin American novelist and one that he treats in many of his works. Incest, as well, would be an important García Márquez theme: Fear of the consequences of an incestuous union contributes to the founding of Macondo, and another incestuous coupling results in its destruction and the end of the Buendía line.

Antigone would have an equally great influence on the young author. *Leaf Storm* begins with a quotation from the Greek tragedy and revolves around the determination of an unnamed colonel to afford a friend a proper burial, against the wishes of the community. *Antigone* would also help the Colombian writer achieve the recognition, central to his fiction, "that no human drama can be unilateral." The play is concerned with the irreconcilable conflict between the obligations owed to the dead and to the community, as dramatized in the conflict between the title character and Creon, the king. "Both sides have spoken well," the play's chorus regularly intones, and in his fiction García Márquez never denies his "villains" the humanity he affords his other characters, though it is clear that he agrees with the character of Luisa Santiaga in *Chronicle of a Death Foretold* that "you always have to take the side of the dead." Likewise, even his "heroes" always have their all-too-human weaknesses.

But the most important reading García Márquez did during this period was of the novels of William Faulkner. References to "the old man," as the Barranquilla Group called the Mississippi novelist, abound in García Márquez's columns from that period, where Faulkner was extolled as the "greatest figure in world literature" and "the most extraordinary and vital creative artist in the modern world." "When I read Faulkner, I discovered I wanted to become a writer," García Márquez would tell Vargas Llosa.

Faulkner's works would exercise their greatest influence on García Márquez by helping awaken in him the realization that it was to his own past that he should look for his literary subject. Faulkner's most important novels and short stories are all set in a fictional Mississippi county of his own creation, Yoknapatawpha, that has many things in common with the costeño world that García Márquez would

Oedipus tries to answer the Sphinx's riddle, in a Greek ceramic painting of the 5th century B.C. *Realizing that his knowledge of fiction was limited to the modern era, García Márquez began to read the classics. The plays of the Greek dramatist Sophocles influenced him profoundly, especially* Oedipus Rex.

transform into Macondo and its environs. Yoknapatawpha had its inspiration, in large part, in the stories
told by and about William Clark Falkner, the novelist's
great-grandfather and a rebel colonel on the losing
side in the civil war that was the defining event in the
region's history. It is a region exploited economically
in the aftermath of its civil war by outsiders, whose
inhabitants nostalgically look back to the glory of the
past rather than toward a meaningful future. It is a
region steeped in violence and economic injustice,
subject to a national government nominally its own
but considered by its residents to be an oppressive,
outside power. Its lifeways constitute a subculture
often regarded contemptuously by the other citizens
of its nation. Its climate is steamy and sultry, almost
tropical. Its landscape is dominated by a great river
that flows to the sea. It is a land of poetry and magic,
defined by the relationship between different races.
The following words, written by Vargas Llosa in
description of the Aracataca of García Márquez's
youth, could apply equally well to Faulkner's Yoknapatawpha:

> The town was assaulted by outlaws, decimated
> by epidemics, ravaged by deluges. . . . Paradise
> and hell belonged to the past, and present reality
> consisted of a limbo made up of poverty, heat,
> and routine. Yet that extinct reality remained
> alive in the memory and imagination of the
> people and it was their best weapon against the
> desolation and emptiness of their present reality.
> . . . Aracataca . . . lived on memory, myths, solitude
> and nostalgia.

Indeed, García Márquez likes to jokingly say, Faulkner
is a Caribbean writer.

For the young García Márquez, struggling to find
his voice as a writer, Faulkner's work served to validate
his own growing recognition—born of el bogotazo, la
violencia, and his return to the Caribbean world of his

youth—that the great fiction he wished to write would have to be created from his own past and the world he knew. What Faulkner's fiction, born of everyday life in his own small, obscure corner of the world, said to García Márquez was that it might be possible for him to create a Colombian Yoknapatawpha from the Caribbean world he had known.

These notions were crystallized for García Márquez as a result of a trip he took with his mother at about this time to sell the sprawling, haunted house where his grandparents had raised him. He was already making notes and sketching out chapters for the work he was tentatively calling *La casa*, though he felt that he "was not yet ready to write a book as big as that." Then, with his mother, he rode the train to Aracataca, where he had not been since the death of his grandfather. "At first," he recalled many years later, with the memory of an accomplished storyteller, "I was very happy with the idea of returning to Aracataca."

> But when we got there, I was staggered. The town had not changed at all. I had the sensation that I had left time, that what had separated me from the town was not distance but *time*. So I walked along the streets with my mother and I realized that she was going through something similar. We walked to the pharmacy, which belonged to people who'd been close friends of the family. Behind the counter sat a lady working on a sewing machine. My mother said, 'How are you, my friend?' When the woman finally recognized her, she stood up, and they embraced and cried for more than a half hour. So I had the feeling that the whole town was dead—even those who were alive. I remembered everyone as they had been before, and now they were dead.

His grandfather's house was in poor repair, overrun by ants, the flowers on the patio long gone, the garden shriveled and dusty, the almond trees tired and barren. The sense of the past intruding upon the

William Faulkner, at work in his Mississippi home in 1955. "When I read Faulkner, I discovered I wanted to become a writer," García Márquez once said. Faulkner's shaping of his Mississippi past in the fictional Yoknapatawpha County inspired García Márquez to translate his own Colombian village experiences into the world of Macondo.

present, of the present passing into history right before his eyes, evoked for García Márquez images of Faulkner's literary world. "The past isn't dead. It isn't even past," the Mississippian once wrote. "I felt that I wasn't really looking at the village," the Colombian recalled, "but I was *experiencing* it as if I were reading it."

It was as if everything I saw had already been written, and all I had to do was sit down and copy what was already there and what I was just reading. For all practical purposes everything had evolved into literature: the houses, the people, and the memories. . . . I know now that only a technique like Faulkner's could have enabled me to write down what I was seeing. The atmosphere, the decadence, the heat in the village were roughly the same as what I had felt in Faulkner. . . . What really happened to me in that trip to Aracataca was that I realized that everything that had occurred in my childhood had a literary value that I was only now appreciating.

A depiction of a cockfight, a popular pastime in rural Latin America. In one of his early novellas, No One Writes to the Colonel, *García Márquez wrote of a husband and wife who risked what little they had on a fighting rooster with prize-winning potential.*

HAPPY AND UNKNOWN

The immediate result of García Márquez's return to Aracataca was an outpouring of energy that resulted in the rapid completion of his first novella, *Leaf Storm*, which was written, he said, "for my friends who were helping me and lending me their books and were very enthusiastic about my work." He has always retained a special fondness for this book, which is the first of his works to be set in Macondo. "It's the most spontaneous, the one I wrote with most difficulty and with fewer technical resources. . . . It seems to me a rather awkward, vulnerable book, but completely spontaneous . . . I know exactly how *Leaf Storm* went straight from my guts onto the paper," he told an interviewer in 1973. Nostalgia lent his recollections of writing the book an objectivity and an affection that he may not always have possessed at the time it was written, for when *Leaf Storm* was rejected in 1952 by the first publisher to whom he submitted it, he simply bound the manuscript up and stuck it in a desk drawer at work. Some friends who had read it rescued it from this oblivion in 1955 and submitted it to another publishing house, and it at last appeared in print.

Leaf Storm is itself in part a story of friendship, albeit of a most unusual kind. Except for those which are recalled by the characters, the events of the story

73

take place on a single afternoon in Macondo, September 12, 1928, a Wednesday, between 2:30 and 3:00 in the afternoon, siesta time. During that half hour, an unnamed former military officer, "old, a Colonel of the Republic, and, to top it off, lame in body and sound in conscience," directs the placing of a corpse, the body of a suicide by hanging, into a coffin; obtains the necessary burial order from the town's mayor—who carries a revolver—by paying a bribe; directs the four Guajiro Indians who work for him to nail the coffin shut; and prepares to step out into the blinding sunlight with the coffin for the long walk to the graveyard, armed only with the mayor's unconvincing assertions "that nothing will happen. . . . I don't even think there's anyone left in town who remembers this." The mayor does admit, however, that "there are some people in the windows. But that's just curiosity."

"I think Macondo is capable of doing anything after what I've seen happen in this century," thinks the colonel. The hanged man is a pariah, and in burying him the colonel is defying the civil authorities, represented by the gun-toting mayor; the spiritual authorities, represented by the ineffectual Father Angel, who wishes to uphold church law forbidding the burial of suicides in sanctified ground; and the entire community, which for 10 years has been waiting for the dead man to die. The hanged man was a doctor, a mysterious stranger with a shadowy past who arrived in Macondo in 1903: just after the conclusion of the War of a Thousand Days, those readers with a knowledge of Colombian history realize—the war is alluded to at the novella's opening—and just before the onset of the leaf storm. Because he arrives bearing a letter of recommendation from the Liberal hero Colonel Aureliano Buendía, he is given a room in the colonel's household, where he lives for eight years. As the town's only physician, he enjoys a grudging respect as a "serious professional man" despite "his brusque manner and disordered ways," though that comes to an end with the arrival of the banana company in Macondo, as his patients abandon him for the clinic established by the company. He closes his practice and shuts himself up in his room and later in the house down the street where he moves with Meme, an Indian servant in the colonel's household.

Deserted by the town in favor of the seductive and short-lived prosperity of the leaf storm, he deserts the town in its hour of need. With the banana company gone and Macondo a "ruined village . . . overrun by armed barbarians, a town in terror which buried its dead in a common grave," violence breaks out on the night of a close, hard-fought election, and a number of townspeople are shot. With no one else to turn to, the wounded are carried on stretchers to the doctor's door, but he refuses to treat them. For the remaining 10 years of his life, the doctor lives in constant fear of being murdered by the townspeople, who eagerly await his death; his impenetrable solitude is broken only once, when he successfully treats the colonel for a stroke that two other doctors have diagnosed as untreatable and terminal. In return, he asks the colonel only "to throw a little earth on me when morning finds me stiff. That's all I need for the buzzards not to eat me." In response, the colonel says, "It's an unnecessary request, doctor. You know me and you must know that I would have buried you over the heads of everybody even if I didn't owe my life to you." Three years later, he cuts the doctor down from the roof beam from which he has hanged himself, and, though believing that "nothing can help my promise in the face of the ferocity of a town and that I'm hemmed in, surrounded by the hatred and impatience of a band of resentful people," prepares to bury the doctor.

The events of September 12, 1928, and the events that led up to them are seen from the alternating points of view, expressed in the first person, of three of

the story's four most important characters—the colonel, his seven-year-old grandson, and his daughter, the
boy's mother. Of the main characters, the only one
whose own point of view is not expressed is arguably
the most important—the doctor. The practice of using shifting first-person points of view is perhaps
Faulkner's most famous narrative technique; omitting
the central character's point of view is also a Faulk-
nerian tactic, utilized most famously in his great novel
The Sound and the Fury.

In *Leaf Storm*, many of the themes that would
come to figure prominently in García Márquez's fiction are evident—the consequences of political violence on life in Colombia's villages, the inability of
Colombia to learn from its past, the duty of individual
conscience in society, individual solitude, the legacy of
outside economic and political interference, the lack
of solidarity among the townspeople. As would be the
case with many of his books, García Márquez would
be criticized for not offering any "solutions" to the
problems he treats in *Leaf Storm*, but he believed then,
as now, that the author's duty is to "describe situations," not prescribe solutions. From the first, he
believes, can come art; from the second, only
"dogma."

In *Leaf Storm*, García Márquez's art is not yet fully
developed. The language of the novella is unique
among his works. Not yet in evidence is the preter-
naturally flowing, translucent, seemingly effortless and
simple, almost oral style that would distinguish *One
Hundred Years of Solitude* and most of García Márquez's
subsequent novels. The language of *Leaf Storm* feels
more worked; it is at times consciously poetic and
sometimes echoes Faulkner's cadences. Nor is the
so-called magical element that is the most readily
identifiable characteristic of *One Hundred Years of Solitude* and some of the later works yet in evidence,
although it is hinted at. García Márquez was still

Musicians playing at a festival in Colombia. When García Márquez was writing his first novella, Leaf Storm, *during the early 1950s, he derived much enjoyment from both his professional and personal life—after working hard all day on his newspaper column and his fiction, he would join his friends for a night of merrymaking.*

searching for his voice, that combination of subject matter, theme, and language that makes a writer's work singular and memorable, but he was justifiably pleased with the progress that *Leaf Storm* represented. "From the moment I wrote *Leaf Storm*," he said many years later as he contemplated the solitude of fame, "I realized I wanted to be a writer and that nobody could stop me and that the only thing left for me to do was to try to be the best writer in the world."

The time when García Márquez wrote his first novella was a period of great personal joy. He was surrounded by friends, doing work—both journalism and fiction—that he loved and was proud of. Afternoons were spent at *El Heraldo*'s offices, writing his column; when he was finished, he would stay on well into the evening working on his fiction, soothed by the noise of the linotype machines, "which sounded like rain. If they stopped, and I was left in silence, I wouldn't be able to work." Then it was on to a café to rendezvous with the Barranquilla group and other friends. Sunrise usually found him as he made his way to his lodgings in El Rascacielos (the Skyscraper), a four-story building on El Calle de Crimen (Crime

Street). The bottom two floors were occupied by law offices; the top two were a brothel. The writer had worked out an arrangement with the prostitutes whereby he was allowed to sleep in whatever room he found vacant. When he was short of money for his lodging, he left the manuscript of *Leaf Storm* as security with the madam. On awaking, he usually ate lunch with the girls, whom he always remembered as having been "real friends" to him at an important time in his life; prostitutes—"solitary women who hate their work"—are always portrayed sympathetically in his work.

In 1953, García Márquez left Barranquilla and his job, for reasons that remain obscure. It seems that he spent most of that year selling encyclopedias in La Guajira with Álvaro Cepeda. In *Chronicle of a Death Foretold*, he writes of "an uncertain period when I was trying to understand something of myself by selling encyclopedias and medical books in the town of Guajira." During his wanderings on the desert peninsula, which would form the setting for several of the stories collected in 1972 as *La increíble y triste historia de la cándida Eréndira y de su abuela desalmada* (The Incredible and Sad Tale of Innocent Erendira and Her Heartless Grandmother), he met the grandson of the man whom his own grandfather had killed in that long-ago duel in Riohacha. Sometime during this period he also became formally engaged to Mercedes Barcha.

The next year he moved to the hated city of Bogotá, where he worked as a staff reporter for *El Espectador*, one of Colombia's two Liberal national daily newspapers. Unlike some writers and critics, who regard journalism as something of a lesser pursuit than fiction—literature's poorer cousin—García Márquez makes no such distinctions and has stated on more than one occasion that he regards journalism as his "true profession." In particular, he has said, he envies its ability to exert a more immediate effect on society than literature, to deal more directly with issues of immediate consequence.

And at this time, García Márquez was certainly giving a great deal of thought to the political situation in Colombia and to his responsibilities as a writer. La violencia was still raging in the countryside, Colombia was ruled by a military dictator, Gustavo Rojas Pinilla, and the young writer wondered whether he did not have an obligation, both in his life and in his work, to attempt to address more directly the problems that were tearing his nation apart. It was at this time that he began some type of brief affiliation with the Colombian Communist party. Though he has continued to believe that socialism offers the best solution for Colombia's problems, it would be misleading to label García Márquez a Communist, for he is too free-minded and critical of dogma to be easily labeled. The best way to describe his politics is to call him an independent leftist who supports those political solutions that allow Colombia (and Latin America) to address its own problems without outside interference, especially from the United States, and that offer its impoverished masses the best means of political and economic empowerment.

Meanwhile, García Márquez managed to run afoul of Colombia's government authorities, but as the result of his most famous journalistic piece, not his political affiliations. In April 1955, *El Espectador* ran a series of 14 articles, one a day for two weeks, collectively entitled "The Truth About My Adventure," signed by Luis Alejandro Velasco, a Colombian sailor who had survived a shipwreck, but actually written by García Márquez, who had conducted extensive interviews with the castaway. Velasco had been serving aboard a Colombian naval vessel that had been

Soldiers guard a Bogotá intersection in 1957 after demonstrations against President Gustavo Rojas Pinilla. After García Márquez wrote a series of articles unmasking government corruption, he left for Europe to protect himself from reprisals.

swamped in high seas while returning to Cartagena from Mobile, Alabama. He and seven companions were swept overboard; all except him drowned. After managing to clamber into a life raft, Velasco survived for 10 days on the open sea without water or food until making a landfall on the Colombian coast, whereupon he was hailed as a national hero—until García Márquez's articles appeared.

The government's explanation of the Velasco affair had been that the sailors had fallen overboard as the result of a freak storm that also made rescue efforts impossible, but as García Márquez's stories made clear to the enthralled and daily increasing readership of *El Espectador*, the truth was somewhat different. The seas had been heavy, it is true, but there had been no storm; the problem was that Velasco's ship had been dangerously overloaded with contraband consumer merchandise, most of which had been insecurely lashed to the deck. It was runaway refrigerators and washing machines, not crashing waves, that swept the sailors overboard, and the overloaded ship, near foundering, was unable to maneuver to effect a rescue. "It was clear that the tale, like the destroyer, also carried an ill-secured political and moral cargo which we had not foreseen," García Márquez wrote in 1970 when the articles were published as a book, *Relato de un naufrago* (The Story of a Shipwrecked Sailor). The Colombian government, already smarting from criticisms by the Liberal press, was not pleased by these revelations. Velasco, a short-lived hero, was drummed out of the navy, and García Márquez was sent to Europe by *El Espectador*'s editors to get him out of the vindictive reach of the Rojas Pinilla government.

As *El Espectador*'s sole European correspondent, "this roving and nostalgic Colombian," as García Márquez would later and famously describe himself, spent several weeks in Geneva, Switzerland; Rome, Italy; Poland; and Hungary before settling in Paris in January 1956. In the City of Light, he found himself a man without a newspaper: news reached him that Rojas Pinilla had shut down *El Espectador* as well as *El Tiempo*, Colombia's other Liberal daily. Instead of returning home, García Márquez cashed in the return ticket the paper had sent him and settled into a garret in the city's Latin Quarter for a period of prolonged work on what would become the novella *No One Writes to the Colonel*.

His time in Paris would be one era of his life that García Márquez would never look back on with nostalgia. He has never been a devotee of the myth of the suffering artist—"I'm very much against the romantic concept of writing which maintains that the act of writing is a sacrifice and that the worse the economic conditions or the emotional state, the better the writing"—and in Paris in 1956 he was poor, lonely, and hungry most of the time. "Poor Gabito," his mother said upon receiving a photograph of himself that he sent her during that time. "He looks like a skeleton." The generosity of his landlady, who let the rent slide for months at a time, and the coins he made from collecting deposit bottles and returning them enabled him to survive, and he somehow managed to maintain enough energy and concentration to complete 11 drafts of *No One Writes to the Colonel*. The version with which he was most pleased, though not satisfied, he tied up with colored ribbon and stuck in a suitcase. Some friends would rescue it in 1961, when it was finally published.

Not surprisingly, the dominant motif in *No One Writes to the Colonel* is hunger. "The colonel took the top off the coffee can and saw that there was only one little spoonful left. He removed the pot from the fire, poured half the water onto the earthen floor, and scraped the inside of the can with a knife until the last scrapings of the ground coffee, mixed with bits of rust, fell into the pot," the story begins. He then generously gives the coffee to his wife, consoling her with the lie that he has already had his.

The colonel is an old man, and it is October—the height of the rainy season in Caribbean Colombia. The rain brings out aches and pains and strange forebodings in the old man. "For nearly sixty years— since the end of the last civil war—the colonel had done nothing but wait. October was one of the few things that had arrived." The colonel, the reader learns later on in the story, is a 75-year-old former compadre of Colonel Aureliano Buendía who has not had "a moment's peace" since the Treaty of Neerlandia. He is also a former resident of Macondo who fled that village with the onset of the banana fever and the coming of the leaf storm.

The period of the colonel's waiting places the story in the present—that is, during the time of la violencia in Colombia. The colonel is up early to dress for a funeral, "the first death from natural causes which we've had in many years." There are other references as well to the unrest in the town: Sabas, the godfather of the colonel's son, is "the only leader of his party who had escaped political persecution and had continued to live in town"; the funeral procession is prevented from passing in front of the police bar-racks, causing Sabas to comment, "I always forget that

García Márquez and the Chilean poet Pablo Neruda strike a comic pose in a Paris garden in 1956. García Márquez suffered from poverty and loneliness during his European exile, but at least he had sympathetic companions such as Neruda—the Chilean had been barred from his own country for three years after criticizing the government.

we are under martial law"; the newspapers are censored. But there are no instances of overt violence in the story. Instead, la violencia seems to lurk just beneath the surface of the story, an event from the past that has shaped the present, a seeming inevitability in the future.

The plot of the story concerns the struggle of the colonel and his wife to survive their rather desperate economic straits, which they endure with humor, stoicism, sarcasm, dignity, hope, and impotent rage. The colonel is awaiting the pension promised him long ago by the government for his service in the War of a Thousand Days; each Friday, he walks to the wharf to await the arrival of the launch that brings the week's mail, only to be told that "no one writes to the colonel." He has been waiting for 19 years.

He and his wife are also mourning for their only son, Agustín, who was shot to death by the police for his political activities. In addition to being beloved by them, Agustín was his parents' sole source of economic support. The only thing of value that he has left them is a prime fighting cock, a potential champion, "the best rooster in the whole province." The game bird is worth a considerable amount of money, but the couple can barely feed themselves, let alone a rooster. The colonel's wife wants him to sell the bird to Sabas, who is the richest man in town (and will pay a high, though unfair, price), but the colonel insists on raising the gamecock, believing that he can win money by betting on it. "You can't eat hope," the woman says. "You can't eat it, but it sustains you," the colonel replies.

More than the hope of future economic gain motivates the colonel in his seemingly foolhardy course of action. "I was thinking that at the Macondo meeting we were right when we told Colonel Aureliano Buendía not to surrender," he says early in the story, and he remains active, in a small way, in the opposition movement. Various gestures of solidarity and compassion sustain him—the doctor gives him his newspapers when he is done reading them and treats him for free, and Agustín's companions help feed the rooster. Nevertheless, the pressure to sell the bird increases as the old couple's poverty deepens and his wife, to her immense shame, is forced to sell household necessities. Still, the colonel holds on to the cock. Sabas, the colonel becomes aware, would resell the rooster at a huge profit, an action that is likened to the rich man's "famous patriotic pact with the Mayor" whereby he gained his fortune by selling the mayor a list of all his comrades in the opposition. The activists were executed or run off, and Sabas took their land. Keeping the rooster becomes for the colonel an act of solidarity, his defense being the argument that all of Agustín's companions, who are still active in the opposition, will bet on the bird.

His wife is uncomprehending. All his vaunted dignity, she tells the colonel—he has never uttered a swear word and "does each thing as if it were a transcendent act"—will not sustain them. "Everybody will win with the rooster except us. We're the only ones who don't have a cent to bet," she tells him, and to his response that the owner of a winning bird is entitled to 20 percent of all the money bet replies, "You were also entitled to a position when they made you break your back for them in the elections. You were also entitled to the veteran's pension after risking your neck in the civil war. Now everyone has his future assured and you're dying of hunger, completely alone."

"I'm not alone," the colonel responds, and though he is unable to explain why not, he feels "pure, explicit, invincible" at the moment when he gives his shocking explanation as to how they will survive the 44 days until the rooster is scheduled to fight.

No One Writes to the Colonel and *In Evil Hour*, the novel that followed it, are the results of García Márquez's decision to directly address the political situation in his country. (*In Evil Hour*, which was also begun while García Márquez was in Paris and continued during his subsequent sojourns in London and Venezuela, is set in the same village as *No One Writes to the Colonel*. Many of the same characters appear—most notably the mayor, Sabas, and the doctor, but not the colonel—and the reader learns much more about them. The plot of the story concerns the mayor's response to an outbreak of "moral terrorism": the appearance of anonymous lampoons, nocturnally posted by "the whole town" and "nobody," that reveal secrets and gossip about the town's rich and powerful and provoke the mayor's armed henchmen into the senseless and brutal execution of an innocent boy that in turn compels an uprising.) Both are stories of la violencia, but García Márquez's approach differs from that of the many other Colombian writers who were then writing about that subject in that he concentrates on the causes and consequences of the violence rather than on cataloging its horrors.

In both stories, la violencia is omnipresent, yet the reader never directly experiences a single killing. Instead, what García Márquez does in *No One Writes to the Colonel* and *In Evil Hour* is to show the effect of la violencia on day-to-day life in Colombia's villages. His emphasis is on the individual and the interpersonal—the doctor and his wife staying up "till dawn, trying to figure out the places and circumstances of the shooting"; the solitude and fear of the mayor, the architect of the terror that permeates the town, "on the dawn when he had disembarked furtively with an old cardboard suitcase tied with cord and the order to make the town submit at all costs"; the colonel, with forbidden literature in his pocket, staring down the rifle-bearing policemen who shot his son; the mayor placing himself, because of the unbearable pain of a toothache, in the hands of his worst political enemy, the dentist, who operates on him without anesthesia "because you people kill without anesthesia"; the consequences for those who seek to maintain their honor and the methods by which others unscrupulously profit from the disturbances. The language used differs from that of *Leaf Storm* and the works still to come; it is stark, realistic, even terse at times.

The subject matter and treatment reflected García Márquez's conviction, coincident with his newfound political commitment, that *Leaf Storm*, which reflected his examination of his own past, constituted an evasion of his responsibility as a writer to address the problems of Colombian society. "After having written *Leaf Storm*," he said some years later, "I decided that writing about the village and my childhood was really an escape from having to face and write about the political reality of my country." His model for the novella, novel, and many of the short stories he was

Ernest Hemingway at work in the early 1930s. Hemingway's work was the main inspiration for No One Writes to the Colonel, *which makes extensive use of Hemingway's "iceberg" theory of storywriting, in which the underlying theme is implied rather than directly stated.*

then writing (which would be collected in *Big Mama's Funeral*) was not Faulkner but Hemingway. A master of terse, realistic prose, Hemingway was a hero to many Latin American writers for his commitment to the republican cause during the Spanish Civil War and for his love of Latin culture (he lived for many years in Cuba), but García Márquez was more interested in his famous "iceberg" theory of storywriting. Hemingway believed that just as an iceberg cruises along with just the smallest part of its bulk visible, while the dangerous mass remains hidden beneath the water, it was possible to write a story "about" a certain theme, through the skillful use of language and the manipulation of information, in a way that never addresses the subject directly yet enables the reader to understand the true topic of the story. His most famous use of this approach is probably the short story "Hills Like White Elephants," which concerns an abortion. *No One Writes to the Colonel* and *In Evil Hour* both make use of this technique in their treatment of la violencia, which permeates the atmosphere of both stories yet is never evoked directly. Its presence in the village is always implied, but rarely stated.

"I considered that the important thing, in terms of literature," said García Márquez,

> was not the inventory of deaths and the description of the methods of violence—which was what the other writers were doing—but what mattered to me, which was the root of that violence, the motives . . . and above all the consequences of that violence for the survivors. That's why you find that in *In Evil Hour* there aren't any killings. The critical period of the violencia is practically over, but what you do see in the book is that the moment of respite hangs by a thread, and that the violencia will return, that it is a kind of constant, that we haven't finished with it because we haven't finished with its causes.

ONE HUNDRED YEARS OF SOLITUDE

The distance of the unnamed village of *No One Writes to the Colonel* and *In Evil Hour* from Macondo can be seen as a metaphor for the distance García Márquez was now feeling from his fiction. A perfectionist and always a harsh critic of his own efforts—"I think that it is a privilege to do anything to a perfect degree"—the author was not satisfied with either book. Both works, García Márquez would come to feel, represented a move away, in both intent and execution, from the great work—the chronicle of the Buendías—that he had begun to envision at about the time he made his return visit to Aracataca. While not renouncing any of his political views, he had misstepped, he came to believe, in attempting a "journalistic literature" that sought to directly address the contemporary problems of his society. As the roots of those problems were in the past, he could use the past—and, specifically, his own past—to illuminate the present:

García Márquez displays his 1982 Nobel Prize during the awards ceremony in Stockholm, Sweden. In his acceptance speech, the Colombian novelist spoke of the Latin American writer's dilemma: How could one find the words to make outsiders understand the grotesque political reality of the continent?

At the time I was twenty-two or twenty-three I had written *Leaf Storm*, I had in my head the glimmerings of *One Hundred Years of Solitude*, and I said to myself: "How can I keep on working in this mythical field and with this poetical style, in the circumstances that we're living through? It

89

seems like an evasion." It was a political decision,
a mistaken one, I now think. I decided to come
nearer to the actuality of the Colombian experience and I wrote *No One Writes to the Colonel*
and *In Evil Hour.* . . . But when I finished *In Evil
Hour,* I saw that all my views were wrong again.
I came to see that in fact my writings about my
childhood were *more* political and had more to
do with the reality of my country than I had
thought. I had an idea of what I always wanted
to do, but there was something missing and I was
not sure what it was until one day I discovered
the right tone—the tone that I eventually used
in *One Hundred Years of Solitude.*

In the meantime, García Márquez had been rescued from his Paris destitution by his old school chum
from Zipaquirá, Plinio Apuleyo Mendoza, who had
secured a position as an editor with *Elite,* a Venezuelan
pictorial newsweekly. Mendoza gave García Márquez
several free-lance assignments, and in late 1957 the
two friends traveled together in the Communist nations of Eastern Europe, visiting Czechoslovakia, Poland, East Germany, Hungary, and the Soviet Union.
García Márquez's accounts of their wanderings appeared in several different Latin American publica-
tions. Though he remained convinced that socialism
was the best solution to Colombia's ills, he was not
uncritical of life as he saw it in the eastern bloc. He
likened the oppression of the populace in East Germany to that in Colombia during the worst days of la
violencia, and he was saddened by the inescapable
realization that communism had not resulted in the
happiness of the masses: "For us it was incomprehensible that the people of East Germany could have
seized power, the means of production, commerce,
banking, communications, and yet could be a sad
people, the saddest people I know." In the Soviet
Union, he viewed the embalmed corpse of Joseph
Stalin, dictator and architect of the death of millions of

Soviet citizens, "plunged in a sleep without remorse."
He noted with fascination the delicacy of Stalin's
hands, a detail he would use in the creation of the
figure of the dictator in *The Autumn of the Patriarch*.

From Eastern Europe, Mendoza returned to Venezuela, García Márquez to poverty in a frigid one-
room flat in rainy London. Rescue came shortly, again
in the person of Mendoza, who mailed Márquez a
plane ticket to Caracas. The journalist had taken a
position as executive editor of *Momento*, another
Venezuelan newsmagazine, and wanted his friend to
join the staff as a writer. García Márquez arrived in
Venezuela on Christmas Eve, 1957, just in time to
witness the celebrations that accompanied the fall of
the nation's dictator, General Marcos Pérez Jiménez,
who fled the country a few weeks later for the United
States, his suitcases stuffed full of American dollars.

In March 1958, the wandering writer visited his
homeland for the first time in nearly three years.
Uncertain of how he would be treated by the authorities, he kept his return quiet and brief, just long
enough to accomplish his purpose: to marry Mercedes Barcha. "This is one of the mysteries of her
personality that will never be clear to me," García
Márquez said to an interviewer in 1983 about Mercedes' steadfastness during his years of wandering.
"She was absolutely certain I'd return. Everyone told
her she was crazy, that I'd find someone new in
Europe. And in Paris, I did lead a totally free life. But I
knew when it was over, I'd return to her. It wasn't a
matter of honor, but more like natural destiny, like
something that had already happened." The writer
returned with his wife to Caracas immediately after
their wedding, but for the newlyweds the rare security
of a paying job was not to last long.

In May 1958, the vice-president of the United
States, Richard Nixon, came to Caracas on an official
visit. For many in Venezuela, resentful of the United

States for providing sanctuary to the hated Pérez Jiménez and for its long history of support for South American dictators and interference in Latin American affairs, Nixon was a most unwelcome guest, as he would have been most places in Latin America. Four years earlier, the U.S. government, at the behest of the United Fruit Company, had arranged the overthrow of the government of the democratically elected president of Guatemala, Jacobo Arbenz Guzmán, who had had the temerity to nationalize the fruit company's unused lands. Many Latin Americans considered the U.S. actions in Guatemala an outrage; for those with a historical perspective, the Guatemala coup was just the most recent in a long legacy of U.S. transgressions in the region.

Nixon was therefore seen as merely the latest representative of Yankee imperialism and was treated accordingly. Huge demonstrations and protests against his visit were held, he was jeered and hooted at during most of his public appearances, and on one occasion university students stoned him and spat upon him. The motorcade that took him from the airport to Caracas was ambushed by a mob, and police intervention was required for his rescue. Both Nixon and the U.S. government chose to regard the incidents as calculated diplomatic insults planned by, in the vice-president's words, "tough Communist agitators."

Faced with President Dwight Eisenhower's implied threat of invasion by marine paratroopers—four divisions were hastily airlifted to the Caribbean—Venezuela's government immediately apologized for the behavior of its citizenry. When the editor-in-chief of *Momento* ran an editorial in the magazine condemning the protests and supporting the United States as "a friendly nation with which we are naturally linked," an appalled García Márquez and Mendoza submitted their resignations.

Now began another spell of wandering for the roving Colombian, this time accompanied by the faithful Mercedes. After a brief stint as the managing editor of a raunchy Caracas tabloid, García Márquez journeyed to Havana, the capital city of Cuba, where with the arrival of the new year 1959 insurgents led by a hirsute guerrilla named Fidel Castro succeeded in overthrowing Fulgencio Batista, the island's spectacularly corrupt, U.S.-supported dictator. Batista was, among other things, the chosen dictator of the North American Mafia, and his encouragement of their business initiatives had helped make Havana Latin America's fleshpot and gambling den, catering to a rich North American clientele. To many Latin Americans, Batista's Cuba was an embarrassment. "Before the Revolution," García Márquez would write, "I never had the curiosity to get to know Cuba. The Latin Americans of my generation thought of Havana as a scandalous gringo brothel."

García Márquez and Mendoza were among a number of prominent Latin American journalists whom Castro invited to Cuba to witness the revolution firsthand. Excited by Castro's attempts to transform Cuban society by eliminating the gross inequities in wealth that had existed under Batista, the two Colombians agreed to establish a Bogotá branch of Castro's news agency, Prensa Latina. The aim was to counter the anti-Castro propaganda put out by the United States, which was appalled by the developments in Cuba. (Castro was a Communist, and Cuba is just 90 miles from Florida; the prospect of a Communist government on its doorstep was just too much for the U.S. government to bear, and in 1961 it even sponsored an invasion aimed at Castro's overthrow. The invasion failed, but since 1961 the United States has not maintained diplomatic or trade relations with Cuba.)

In May 1958, the motorcade of U.S. vice-president Richard Nixon was attacked in Caracas, Venezuela, by demonstrators protesting U.S. support for Latin American dictators. García Márquez resigned his editorial post when his magazine, Momento, condemned the demonstrations.

Working 16-hour shifts, the two friends succeeded in establishing the Bogotá office on a solid footing. For García Márquez, it was an exceptionally busy time; his first son, Rodrigo, was born on August 24, 1959, and was baptized by another old friend, Camilo Torres. Not long after the baby was born, the young family moved to New York City, where García Márquez ran the North American branch of Prensa Latina. Communists were not especially popular in the United States, and he received frequent death threats. When ideological rifts within the Communist party in Cuba resulted in the resignation from Prensa Latina of Jorge Massetti, the man who had hired García Márquez and Mendoza, the two Colombians resigned as well.

Mercedes was gathering experience that would serve her well in the future when her husband would retreat to the Cave of the Mafia; she had become expert in packing quickly, establishing households in a variety of locations, and making do on little or no money. Unemployed and nearly broke—he had $100 in his pocket, and another $120, wired by Mendoza, was waiting at the Colombian consulate in New Orleans—Gabo, Mercedes, and the baby, Rodrigo, boarded a Greyhound bus at the Port Authority Bus Terminal on New York City's West Side. Their destination was Mexico City, where García Márquez had a vague promise of work writing screenplays, but he was more excited about the going than the getting-there: The bus's route would take them through the heart of Faulkner country in Mississippi. "I traveled by bus because I wanted to see the small, dusty roads that Faulkner described," the pilgrim remembered in 1983, "and also because I had almost no money. I saw a world very similar to my hometown of Aracataca in Colombia. As a company town built by United Fruit, Aracataca had the same wooden shacks with roofs made of zinc and tin. In Faulkner's country I remember seeing the small stores along the roadway with people seated out front with their feet up on railings. There was the same kind of poverty contrasting with great wealth."

Though Mexico City would be the closest thing García Márquez has had to a home since leaving Aracataca at the age of eight, his first years there were not especially happy ones. Although a couple of his screenplays did make it to the screen, most of his work in that genre remained unproduced. The several short stories he had written since finishing *In Evil Hour*—considered by at least one critic, upon their publication as *Big Mama's Funeral* in 1967, as "among the most perfect instances of the genre ever written in Latin America"—did not ease the frustration he felt at being unable to progress on the great novel of Macondo. The publication of *In Evil Hour* proved to be a disaster: A copy editor took it upon him- or herself to correct all slang, eliminate all obscenities, and otherwise rewrite the book. García Márquez was so offended by the published version that he repudiated it. The arrival of his second son, Gonzalo, on April 16, 1962, added to his sense of responsibility and growing conviction that he was a failure. To his despair, he found himself unable to write any more fiction, and he took a job with an advertising agency.

Then came the epiphany in the Opel on the highway from Mexico City to Acapulco in January 1965. The way to write his book was now clear to him; it was Kafka's way, but most of all it was his grandmother's way. "The tone that I eventually used in *One Hundred Years of Solitude*," its author has stated,

> was based on the way my grandmother used to tell her stories. She told things that sounded supernatural and fantastic, but she told them with complete naturalness. . . . What was most important was the expression she had on her face. She did not change her expression at all when telling her stories and everyone was surprised. In previous attempts to write *One Hundred Years of Solitude*, I tried to tell the story without believing in it. I discovered that what I had to do was believe in them myself and write them with the same expression with which my grandmother told them: with a brick face.

Gabo retired to the Cave of the Mafia, and Mercedes took over the family's affairs. Eighteen months later, *One Hundred Years of Solitude* was completed, and a literary earthquake rocked Latin America.

The marriage of the mundane and the marvelous is the most striking aspect of *One Hundred Years of Solitude*. The basic history of Macondo, as related in the novel, will not, however, seem strange to any reader with some knowledge of Colombian and Latin American history. The village is founded by several families, foremost among them the Buendías, after a journey across the mountains. Its innocence—and isolation—is shattered by the arrival of Europeans (gypsies in the novel) bearing esoteric knowledge and Old World gadgets; for the first time, Macondo becomes aware of its solitude. A representative of the central government and later a contingent of soldiers is sent to the town; their corruption, oppression, and brutality transform Macondo, hitherto "a town with no political passions" into a Liberal stronghold and

Cuban revolutionary leader Fidel Castro waves to a cheering crowd upon his arrival in Havana on January 1, 1959, as dictator Fulgencio Batista fled the island. Castro soon invited García Márquez, by then well known as a journalist, to witness the Cuban Revolution firsthand.

Aureliano Buendía into an unconquerable rebel colonel. The civil wars end with the defeat of the Liberals and the arrival, soon afterward, of the American banana company, which transforms Macondo almost beyond the recognition of its longtime inhabitants. Various outrages on the part of the banana company lead to the murder by unknown assassins—after his vainglorious threat to arm "my boys" and resume the war—of all the 17 sons fathered by Colonel Buendía with 17 different women during the civil wars, a strike, and then a hideous massacre of the workers and their families by government troops in an open square near the Macondo train station, but no one believes José Arcadio Segundo Buendía's subsequent eyewitness testimony about the killings. The banana company promises to negotiate with its workers but pulls out of Macondo instead, leaving behind a ruined village that will never recover. The reader learns this larger history of Macondo through his or her involvement with the individual fortunes of the various Buendías, and the novel is as concerned with the private lives of these characters—their marriages, friendships, love affairs, rivalries, children, and so on—as it is with national events.

Throughout the novel, interspersed with its recognizable historical events and the mundane occurrences of day-to-day private life, are a number of seemingly incredible happenings. A priest levitates while drinking chocolate; a virginal beauty ascends into heaven while hanging out the wash to dry; gypsies zoom about on flying carpets; it rains for 4 years, 11 months, and 2 days following the massacre of the striking workers; a cloud of yellow butterflies accompanies a garage mechanic wherever he goes; several individuals return from the dead; a "silent storm" of "tiny yellow flowers . . . so many that in the morning the streets were covered with a compact cushion and they had to clear them away with shovels and rakes so that the funeral procession could pass by" rains gently down on the death of the first José Arcadio Buendía; the village is bedeviled by a plague of insomnia, in which loss of memory accompanies sleeplessness; a rivulet of blood from a slain son traces a path to his mother's door.

All are narrated in the same tone and voice as the other events in the novel; no explanations or justifications of their implausibility are given, aside from an accumulation of accompanying detail, a narrative trick, intended to enhance credibility, that García Márquez learned from his grandmother, Kafka, and his days as a journalist. For example, it does not rain for "a long time" after the massacre; it rains for precisely 4 years, 11 months, and 2 days. "The tricks you need to transform something which appears fantastic, unbelievable into something plausible, credible, those I learned from journalism; the key is to tell it straight. It is done by reporters and country folk," García Márquez has said. "If you say that there are elephants flying in the sky, people are not going to believe you. But if you say that there are four hundred and twenty-five elephants in the sky, people will probably believe you. That's a journalistic trick which you can also apply to literature. *One Hundred Years of Solitude* is full of that sort of thing. That's exactly the technique my grandmother used."

The seamless blend of the fantastic and the realistic achieved by García Márquez in *One Hundred Years of Solitude* has been termed magical realism. The author does not like the term because he believes that it emphasizes the fantastic at the expense of what he is trying to say about the reality of life in Latin America. "Every single line in *One Hundred Years of Solitude*, in all my books, has a starting point in reality," he argues. "I provide a magnifying glass so readers can understand reality better." The magical events recounted in *One Hundred Years of Solitude* are presented not to convince the reader that such things happen in Macondo, but to illuminate a world whose inhabitants, like the people García Márquez had known in Aracataca in his childhood, understand or interpret reality in a way that accepts the possibility of such events occurring. *One Hundred Years of Solitude* is the history of Macondo and the Buendías as it might have been understood and told by García Márquez's grandmother, had she the skill of a born storyteller, the knowledge of the studied novelist, and the genius of a literary master.

Such happenings may be fantastic, but so, the novel tells us, is the "reality" of the past and present in Macondo (and Latin America). It may be difficult, for example, for a reader to believe that a stunningly beautiful, naked young woman could be carried aloft and away by a soft afternoon breeze, but it is also difficult to believe that a governmental massacre could be so successfully covered up that its very occurrence could be left open to question, or that "the banana company did not have, never had had, and never would have any workers in its service" and that a "decision of the court" would establish by "solemn decrees that the workers did not exist," or that, as does

Colonel Aureliano Buendía, a soldier could lead 32 rebellions and lose them all. And yet, in "reality," the massacre of the banana workers was covered up, a court did rule that the United Fruit Company had no workers, and the unsuccessful uprisings of the Liberal party are too numerous to count. The point made by the novel is that the reality of life in Latin America, both past and present, in both an individual and historical context, is fantastic, and it is the inability of outsiders to comprehend that reality, their lack of interest in doing so, and their unwillingness to let Latin America chart its own singular destiny that has in large part condemned the region to its seemingly inescapable solitude.

Chilean President Salvador Allende. When Allende, a democratically elected Socialist, was killed in a right-wing coup in 1973, García Márquez wrote a detailed and scathing magazine article condemning the U.S. government for its role in engineering the coup.

Solitude is, of course, the most important theme of the novel. "To interpret *One Hundred Years of Solitude* as meaning 'no one will ever know us' is correct," García Márquez has said. "*Everyone* is afraid of solitude. When you open your eyes in the morning, the first feeling is always fright." The characters of the novel experience many different kinds of solitude. All eventually suffer the solitude of death; for some, their nostalgia for life is too great, and they return to the land of the living. Úrsula Buendía, the family's tireless matriarch, experiences the solitude of motherhood and love in enduring the death of her husband and several children and grandchildren, and then the solitude of an old age in which it is difficult for others to even tell whether she is dead or alive. Amaranta Buendía experiences the solitude of lovelessness because of her cold heart. Several of the male characters sentence themselves to solitude in the obsessive pursuit of knowledge. Colonel Aureliano Buendía experiences the solitude of power when too many years of war turn him, briefly, into a tyrant.

The village of Macondo also experiences several kinds of solitude. Immediately after its founding, it is isolated geographically, unknown by the rest of the world and largely unknowing of it. After the arrival of the gypsies, the village experiences the solitude of believing itself backward and unsophisticated in comparison with the Old World. The civil wars bring another form of solitude, as they divide countrymen and even family members from one another, as do the leaf storm and the banana fever. Later, Macondo knows the solitude of abandonment after the banana company, having rendered the village dependent and helpless, removes its operation. Aside from its founding, the entire history of the village is one of solitude, in that its destiny is almost always decided by outsiders.

"To the Europeans, South America is a man with a mustache, a guitar, and a gun," wrote García Márquez in *No One Writes to the Colonel*. "They don't understand the problem." European assumptions about Latin America infuriated him during the time when he was a struggling writer in the Old World, as did North American misconceptions in the years that followed. How can you live in such savage countries as exist in South America, where people kill one another for political reasons, he would be asked. The question made him "furious." "Our countries are only 170 years old," he would reply.

> European countries are much older than that and have gone through far more atrocious episodes than what we in Latin America are going through. That we should seem savage to them now! We have never had as barbarian a revolution as the French Revolution! The Swiss— cheesemakers who consider themselves great pacifists—were Europe's bloodiest mercenaries in the Middle Ages! Europeans had to go through long periods of bloodshed and violence to become what they are today. When we are as old as the European countries, we'll be much

more advanced than Europe is now, because we will have both our experience and theirs to draw upon.

This failure of understanding has been Latin America's historical destiny since its "discovery" by the bold mariners and bloody conquistadores of Spain and is the essence of its solitude. In the speech he gave upon accepting the Nobel Prize for literature in 1982, García Márquez recapitulated Latin American history, from discovery to the present. (The story of Macondo, in metaphor, does the same.) He emphasized the seemingly fantastic tales written by the first explorers of the region in an attempt to impart the wonder and strangeness of this New World, for which their own experience and vocabulary left them unprepared. (*One Hundred Years of Solitude* begins at a time when "the world was so recent [or new] that many things lacked names, and in order to indicate them it was necessary to point," and García Márquez has commented many times that Columbus's journals of his New World travels are the first works of magical realism.) He spoke of the gold fever with which the region's fantastic resources of natural wealth infected its conquerors. He reiterated the incredible outrages and oppressions conceived by its dictators in the years after the region achieved its independence from Spain, and the "strange unearthly tidings from Latin America" in the 11 years since another one of its writers, the Chilean poet Pablo Neruda, had been honored with the Nobel Prize: "A Promethean president, entrenched, alone, in his burning palace, died fighting an entire army" (Chile's Salvador Allende, who was overthrown by a coup planned and sponsored by the government of U.S. president Richard Nixon); the death, under mysterious circumstances, "of another great-hearted president and of a democratic soldier who had restored the dignity of his people" (Panama's Omar Torrijos, killed in a helicopter crash in 1981);

A detail of a 16th-century French map of South America, featuring European conceptions of the New World. "To the Europeans, South America is a man with a mustache, a guitar, and a gun," García Márquez wrote in No One Writes to the Colonel.

"five wars and seventeen military coups"; "the first Latin American ethnocide of our time"; the death of 20 million Latin American children, from poverty and neglect, before the age of one; the "disappearance," without explanation, of 120,000 citizens into Argentina's jails; the death of 200,000 men and women throughout the continent "because they, fighting, wanted not to see their world continue, unchanged"; the flight into exile of thousands more because of their opposition to injustice in their nations.

Such a reality, said García Márquez on that day, which "lives within us" and "sustains the source of the insatiable creativity, full of sorrow and beauty, of which this roving and nostalgic Colombian" has been "singled out by fortune," presents the Latin American writer—and, indeed, "all creatures of that unbridled reality," be they "poets or beggars"—with a special problem. "We have had to ask very little of our imagination," the laureate said, "as our greatest problem has been the inadequacy of a convention or means by which to render our lives believable. This, my friends, is the crux of our solitude."

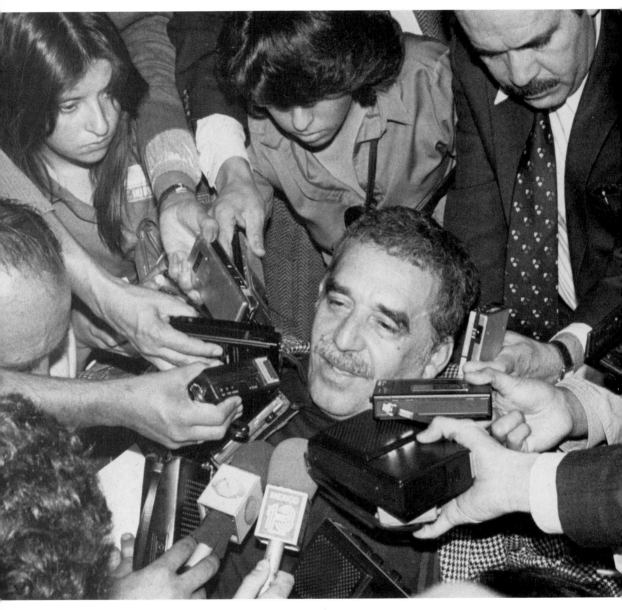

García Márquez is engulfed by reporters in Mexico City in 1981. International success and the Nobel Prize have brought García Márquez political influence. World leaders, such as France's president, François Mitterrand, are known to consult with him on matters concerning Latin America.

THE SOLITUDE
OF FAME

The first readers of *One Hundred Years of Solitude* recognized immediately that García Márquez had done more than any writer before him to render their lives believable and thus dispel Latin America's solitude. A recounting of any nation's history, in its emphasis on the important events and the great men and women of a particular time, often overlooks the impact of such events on those affected by them, but García Márquez's focus is always on the individual, the personal, the familial. Although the author professes to be baffled by the novel's exceptional popularity—"I knew it would be a book that would please my friends more than my others had"—he suggests that one explanation "is that it is a book about the private lives of the people of Latin America, a book that is written from the inside." To the extent that the book is a kind of history, Gene Bell-Villada points out, it is history "from below"—the emphasis is on the people, not their leaders. "There is an underlying tone of irreverence toward officialdom," Bell-Villada writes. The perspective is that of "ordinary townsfolk who find themselves set upon by powerful forces and who, through struggle, play, and eroticism, through work, esoteric studies, and just living, somehow resist."

The book's phenomenal popularity, both in the Spanish-speaking world and elsewhere, ensured that Latin America would be a little less solitary. For García Márquez, the popularity of the book in Latin America was more important than its international success. One consequence of the long history of outside interference in the region had been that serious readers in Colombia and Latin America, like García Márquez himself as a young man, had long looked to Europe and the United States for their literature. That began to change with the publication of *One Hundred Years of Solitude*, whose author feels that the book's most important achievement may be in inspiring Latin Americans to read the literature of their own region.

García Márquez's book is generally regarded as the major catalyst for what has become known as "the boom": an explosion of interest, both in the region and elsewhere, especially the United States, in the literature of Latin America. Suddenly, it seemed, the books of many significant Latin American fiction writers, many of whom had been doing important work for a long time—Mario Vargas Llosa of Peru, Julio Cortázar and Jorge Luis Borges of Argentina, Alejo Carpentier of Cuba, Machado de Assis of Brazil, Carlos Fuentes of Mexico, and José Donoso of Chile, to name several—were being rewarded with unprecedented attention both at home and abroad. "It was discovered that Latin American novels existed which were good enough to be translated and considered with all world literature," García Márquez said in 1981. "What was really sad is that cultural colonialism is so bad in Latin America that it was impossible to convince Latin Americans themselves that their own novels were good until people outside *told* them that they were." The discovery of Latin American literature, both by outsiders and the people of Latin America, was a crucial step toward ending the region's solitude, García Márquez believes.

But the extraordinary success of his novel meant a new kind of solitude for García Márquez. Writing is, of course, a solitary endeavor, and García Márquez had ample experience with the solitude of obscurity, but now he experienced what he termed the solitude of fame. The days of scuffling were over; he was now a public figure, deluged with fan mail, requests for interviews, and myriad presumptions on his time. Though grateful for the material success he has achieved, and for the platform to speak out on political issues that his renown has afforded him, the writer has remained steadfastly wary of fame, which he regards as a tremendously destructive force "because it invades your private life. It takes away from the time you spend with friends, and the time that you can work. It tends to isolate you from the real world. A famous writer who wants to continue writing has to be constantly defending himself against fame."

García Márquez's defense was to plunge himself back into his work and to remove himself from Latin America. His newest obsession was a novel about a Caribbean dictator. As he had himself never lived under a dictatorship for any significant period of time, he moved, with his family, to Barcelona, Spain, to write the book. Spain was then in the last years of the repressive regime of Francisco Franco, who had installed himself in power in 1939 after winning, with the aid of Nazi Germany, a brutal civil war against the nation's elected government.

The Autumn of the Patriarch took García Márquez seven years to write and was published in 1975. It is his most difficult and ambitious novel and the one of which he is most proud, though at the time of its appearance many writers and critics, expecting something more along the lines of *One Hundred Years of Solitude*, pronounced themselves disappointed with it. In years since, however, it has acquired the stature of a minor classic. The kaleidoscopic story of the reign of an ancient dictator of a fictional Caribbean nation—his age is somewhere between 107 and 232—who is equal parts the product of the author's prodigious imagination and a composite of the life and times of the many real-life monsters who have ruled in Latin America since it attained its independence, *The Autumn of the Patriarch* is, according to its author, a "poem on the solitude of power."

It is divided into six sections, each successive one consisting of a lesser number of sentences, so that the final section, forty-some pages in length, consists of just one sentence: the text is not divided into paragraphs. The intention of García Márquez's method is to capture the shifting nature of truth and reality in a nation ruled by such a dictator—"the only mythological figure that Latin America has produced"—where there are, as the novel indicates, always several versions of the truth: the official version, promulgated by the government, is almost always at variance with the truth as lived and experienced by the people. There is even a third version, to which, ironically, the patriarch becomes increasingly susceptible as his absolute power over every aspect of his nation's society grows: the version prepared by his cabinet ministers and courtiers to deceive and placate him.

As his power grows, the patriarch becomes more and more isolated; none dare tell him the truth, and his every wish is anticipated. Thus, the patriarch reads a newspaper, prepared, without his knowing, for his eyes only, in which even the censored news released to the public has been censored to meet his approval; when he leaves his tumbledown palace to inspect his kingdom, he sees evidence everywhere of the progress he

The Fascist dictator of Spain, Francisco Franco (1892–1975). To research The Autumn of the Patriarch, *a novel about a Caribbean dictator, García Márquez went to live in Franco's Spain so he could have the experience of actually living under a dictatorship.*

has decreed, but he is unaware that the magnificent new high-rise apartment buildings are simply facades thrown up over the age-old slums, to be removed once he retreats back into his solitude; the crowds who line the way as his train or carriage passes by, whose presence he regards as approbation of his rule, have been forced into attendance, without his knowledge, by his security forces. Even his perverted love life is a sham; the schoolgirl with whom he falls in love is in reality a young prostitute procured for him by his ministers. In this way, his absolute power ultimately condemns him to absolute solitude, as all his experiences, and the emotions that derive from them, become ultimately, in one way or another, illusory. For in the end the ageless, ancient patriarch, for all his low cunning, casual brutality, unbounded power, and fabulous wealth battened from the nation's treasury, is defeated by his solitude, as he recognizes in the moments before his death that "he had arrived without surprise at the ignominious fiction of commanding without power, of being exalted without glory and of being obeyed without authority." He had sought to compensate for the "infamous fate" of his "incapacity to love" with the "burning cultivation of the solitary vice of power," but triumph in the end rests with the "uncountable years of misfortune" and "ungraspable instants of happiness" of the people, "where love was contaminated by seeds of death but was all love anyway."

Upon the publication of *The Autumn of the Patriarch*, García Márquez declared that he would write no more fiction until the fall from power of General Augusto Pinochet, the strongman who, with the connivance of the United States, had seized power in Chile from the democratically elected socialist president, Salvador Allende, in a military coup in 1973. There followed a long period of political activism. The

writer returned with Mercedes and their two children
to Mexico City, where he purchased a spacious house,
with a studio bungalow out back, in one of its older
suburbs. Other earnings from his books, specifically
prize money won by *One Hundred Years of Solitude* in
Italy, France, Venezuela, and England, was earmarked
for political causes. He donated large sums to a socialist party in Venezuela and to a committee devoted to
the release of political prisoners throughout Latin
America. He contributed articles to newspapers and
magazines on the struggle of Angola to free itself from
Portuguese rule, the Sandinista revolution in Nicara-
gua, and the abuses of the military junta in Argentina.
His friendships with many of Latin America's political
leaders, made possible by the fame he had earned as a
result of his writings, enabled him to act as something
of an extraordinary diplomat with the power and
willingness to intercede in human rights cases. With
his friend Graham Greene, the great English novelist,
García Márquez secured the release of a British banker
kidnapped by Salvadoran guerrillas, and he was asked
by Panama's leader, Omar Torrijos, to serve as an
official member of the Panamanian delegation at the

In the 1980s, Argentinean mothers regularly assembled at the Plaza de Mayo in Buenos Aires to protest the "disappearance" of their children and to demand an accounting for them by Argentina's government. García Márquez consistently used his influence to champion the cause of human rights and social justice in Latin America.

signing of the treaty with the United States that restored control over the Panama Canal to Panama. In Colombia, he founded a newsmagazine, *Alternativa*, which published from 1974 to 1980 and was just the most recent of several attempts he had made over the years to found periodicals that would provide an alternative to Colombia's official press. It accepted no advertising and sought to provide an outlet for a broad array of leftist political and cultural thought, a mission that made its office the target of several terrorist attacks and finally forced its closing.

The most controversial of García Márquez's political activities has been his ongoing friendship with Fidel Castro. In the United States, especially, which has sought to keep Cuba in diplomatic and economic quarantine since Castro came to power in 1961, many have found it incomprehensible that the author of such eloquent examinations of the abuses of power would maintain relations with a person whom they regard as the personification of a totalitarian dictator. García Márquez, of course, sees the situation quite differently. He regards the Cuban Revolution as being of great importance in the history of Latin America in that it represents one of the few instances whereby a Latin American nation has been able to chart its own course completely independent of outside interference. The United States saw in Castro a Communist, beholden to if not controlled by the Soviet Union; García Márquez saw a nationalist, forced by the hostility of its nearest neighbors and natural allies to seek the aid of the Soviet Union. He is aware of the failures of the revolution there; part of his time after the publication of *The Autumn of the Patriarch* was spent writing what he describes as a "very harsh, very frank book" about life in Cuba under Castro. The book has never been published because García Márquez feels that in the United States, where he enjoys an enormous readership, the general anti-Communist hysteria of the political climate, which he believes worsened under the Reagan and Bush administrations, would preclude its being received objectively and would do enormous harm to Cuba. Should the United States normalize relations with Cuba, thus easing its economic insecurity, he will publish the book.

But the real basis of his friendship with Castro, García Márquez has always maintained, is the same as the basis of all his old friendships: literature. The Cuban leader is a voracious reader, and García Márquez brings him a suitcase filled with books each time he visits the island. They rarely discuss politics, the Colombian says (though he concedes that the subject is to some extent inescapable), and their friendship was sealed after Castro stayed up all one night reading *Dracula*, which is one of García Márquez's favorite books. "Gabriel, you screwed me!" the only Communist leader in the western hemisphere exclaimed the next morning. "That book; I couldn't get a minute's sleep." According to García Márquez, Castro is an exceptionally skilled reader, the equal of any editor: the writer even gave him a manuscript of *Chronicle of a Death Foretold* to review for errors and internal contradictions. The friendship is also based on a shared love of good food; Castro "knows everything there is to know about seafood," says García Márquez, who has confessed that eating is the sensuous pleasure that matters most to him.

Harmless as García Márquez would make the friendship, it has caused him, along with his other political activities, a great deal of difficulty. Until 1971, he was not allowed to enter the United States at all; that year Columbia University granted him an honorary degree, and he was allowed to enter the United States for extremely short visits, at the sole discretion

García Márquez visits with Cuban premier Fidel Castro during the 1980s. The author's friendship with the Communist dictator, based more on a mutual love of literature and food than on politics, has caused both the U.S. and Colombian governments to view him with suspicion.

of the State Department. Though the situation has eased somewhat since he received the Nobel Prize in 1982, the world's greatest living writer is still not a welcome guest in the United States, a situation that he finds extremely troubling since, as he puts it, "no cultured man can exist today without traveling frequently to the U.S."

His political associations have also caused García Márquez trouble in his homeland. Though his permanent residence is in Mexico City, since 1975 García Márquez has returned regularly to Colombia, often for months at a time. Shortly before the publication in 1981 (the Pinochet dictatorship having outlived his need to write) of *Chronicle of a Death Foretold*, his fictionalized account of the honor slaying of his friend in Sucre in the 1940s, he fled Colombia, asking for and receiving political asylum in Mexico. He had just returned from a visit with Castro, only to learn that Colombia's Conservative administration had targeted him as an alleged supporter and financier of M-19, a guerrilla group then fighting in the countryside against the government. Captive guerrillas were tortured to provide statements implicating the writer, whose flight and subsequent statements were a source of considerable embarrassment to the government.

That embarrassment multiplied in October of the following year when García Márquez was awarded the Nobel Prize for literature, but the reaction in much of the rest of Latin America was jubilation. Crowds of celebrants poured into the streets of Colombia's cities and villages to dance and party when the announcement was made. GABO NOBEL DE LITERA-TURA read the headline of the nation's leading daily newspaper. *Vallenato* songs (narrative-style ballads of the Caribbean region of Colombia) were composed about him, celebrating his accomplishment. In Mexico City, the entire student body of an elementary school in his neighborhood walked to his house and serenaded him with a song. That night, when he went

García Márquez in Paris with his wife, Mercedes, and his son Gonzalo shortly before winning the Nobel Prize. When the award was announced, the news was greeted with jubilation throughout Latin America.

out for a drive in his BMW, fellow motorists honked at him to gain his attention, then nodded in solemn recognition of his achievement. When his car stalled at a stoplight, he was affectionately chided: "Hey, Gabo, the only thing you're good for is getting the Nobel Prize."

"All of Colombia will be keeping Gabo company," said the nation's new president, Belisario Betancur, who welcomed the laureate back to his homeland and then personally saw him off on the flight to Stockholm, Sweden, where the prize is awarded. Although he hates speaking in public, García Márquez's moving address was an enormous success. His evocation of the solitude of Latin America culminated in a plea for patience and understanding from the richer and more powerful nations, a willingness to concede to Latin America the same originality in its difficult quest for an identity and social justice that was being honored in its literature, and the speech concluded with an homage to another Nobel laureate, "my master, William Faulkner." In his address, the Colombian pointed out, the Mississippian had said, "I decline to accept the end of man." The duty of writers, "the inventors of tales, who will believe anything," García Márquez now proclaimed, is to create "a new and sweeping utopia of life, where no one will be able to decide for others how they die, where love will prove true and happiness be possible, and where the races condemned to one hundred years of solitude will have, at last and forever, a second chance on earth." The week-long festivities concluded with a party at which 60 artists from various Colombian music and dance ensembles performed; García Márquez, dressed in a traditional white linen suit of the Colombian Caribbean, danced with Mercedes; and exquisite Cuban rum, sent by Castro, flowed freely. "Never in all my years with the Nobel organization have I seen the Swedes in so vibrant a mood," the coordinator of events exulted.

"I think that for me it would be an absolute catastrophe," García Márquez had said in 1981 about the prospect of receiving the Nobel Prize. Though it may have increased his apprehensions about the solitude of fame, the prize has proved anything but. His next novel, *Love in the Time of Cholera*, which was published in 1985, is one of his most charming, popular, and accomplished works. In part a retelling of the courtship of his parents, it is a love story set in the Colombian Caribbean before his birth, where love does prove true and happiness is possible. *The General in His Labyrinth*, which was published in 1990, is García Márquez's fictional recreation of the last voyage of Simón Bolívar, the Liberator, who freed Latin America from Spanish rule but whose dream of a united Latin American state, from Central America to Cape Horn, was destroyed by personal and political rivalries and regional factionalism. Both novels return García Márquez to the world of his and Colombia's past, which is used by him, as always, to illuminate the present; both are the works of an assured master of fiction working with complete confidence.

There will be more to come. Although he devotes an increasing amount of time to other interests—politics, of course; the direction of a school of Latin American cinema in Cuba; the writing of screenplays; producing a weekly television newsmagazine show in Bogotá—García Márquez remains at heart a writer of fiction. His discipline remains legendary among his friends; whether at his home in Mexico City or his other residences in Cuernavaca, Paris, Barcelona, or Barranquilla, he rises early most days to write, usually at six, and stays at it until midafternoon. Though he claims that "what I like best is the world of *farandula*, of show business, nightlife . . . staying up all night,

García Márquez in 1991, teaching a class at a school for future filmmakers in Cuba. Although he has branched out into screen-writing and television news, he still devotes his mornings to fiction. "The only thing I ever wanted to do is write," he has often stated.

going to all sorts of parties," he admits that "then I couldn't write. And the only thing I ever wanted to do is write." Believing that "you have to be in almost athletic condition to write every day," he has made concessions to the advancing years by giving up smoking and drinking; the paunch that has developed on his five-foot-nine-inch frame is combated with an exercise bicycle and swimming. Ecstatic over his dis-covery, in the early 1980s, of the powers of the word processor, which has enabled him to write much more quickly than in the past, he is confident that his best work is yet to come. Whenever he is asked what he envisions himself doing on some date in the future, his answer is always the same: "Writing a novel."

CHRONOLOGY

1928   Born Gabriel José García Márquez on March 6, in Aracataca, Colombia

1936   Returns to Sucre, Colombia, to live with his parents

1940   Wins scholarship to the Liceo Nacional, a school for gifted students, in Zipaquirá

1947   Enters the Universidad Nacional in Bogotá; publishes his first story in the newspaper *El Espectador*

1948   Liberal party leader Jorge Eliécer Gaitán is assassinated in Bogotá; García Márquez moves to Cartagena and begins his career as a journalist

1949   Revisits Aracataca and transforms childhood memories into his first novel, *Leaf Storm*

1954   Moves back to Bogotá to work as a reporter for *El Espectador*

1955   Writes a series of articles that anger the government; his employers send him to Europe to protect him from reprisals

1956   Settles in Paris and begins work on *No One Writes to the Colonel* and *In Evil Hour*

1958   Marries Mercedes Barcha, after an 18-year courtship

1959   Visits Cuba to observe the Cuban Revolution;
             establishes branch of Cuban news agency,
             Prensa Latina, in Bogotá; son Rodrigo is born;
             García Márquez sets up Prensa Latina office in
             New York and then moves his family to Mexico
             City

1962   Second son, Gonzalo, is born

1965   Begins work on *One Hundred Years of Solitude*,
             which he completes in 18 months, working
             every day

1967   First edition of *One Hundred Years of Solitude* is
             published in June; the novel sells 500,000 copies
             in Latin America in the next three years and
             becomes an international best-seller

1974   García Márquez founds *Alternativa*, a
             newsmagazine, in Colombia

1975   *The Autumn of the Patriarch* is published

1981   *Chronicle of a Death Foretold* is published

1982   García Márquez wins the Nobel Prize for
             literature

1985   *Love in the Time of Cholera* is published

1987   Worldwide sales of *One Hundred Years of Solitude*
             reach 30 million copies

1989   *The General in His Labyrinth* is published

Further Reading

Bell-Villada, Gene H. *García Márquez: The Man and His Work*. Chapel Hill: University of North Carolina Press, 1990.

Bloom, Harold, ed. *Gabriel García Márquez*. New York: Chelsea House, 1989.

Dreyfus, Claudia. "*Playboy* Interview: Gabriel García Márquez." *Playboy*, February 1983.

García Márquez, Gabriel. *The Autumn of the Patriarch*. Translated by Gregory Rabassa. New York: Harper & Row, 1976.

————. *Chronicle of a Death Foretold*. Translated by Gregory Rabassa. New York: Knopf, 1982.

————. *Collected Stories*. Translated by Gregory Rabassa and J. S. Bernstein. New York: Harper & Row, 1984.

————. *The General in His Labyrinth*. Translated by Edith Grossman. New York: Knopf, 1990.

————. *In Evil Hour*. Translated by Gregory Rabassa. New York: Harper & Row, 1979.

————. *Leaf Storm and Other Stories*. Translated by Gregory Rabassa. New York: Harper & Row, 1972.

————. *Love in the Time of Cholera*. Translated by Edith Grossman. New York: Knopf, 1988.

————. *No One Writes to the Colonel*. Translated by J. S. Bernstein. New York: Harper & Row, 1968.

————. *One Hundred Years of Solitude*. Translated by Gregory Rabassa. New York: Avon, 1979.

————. *The Story of a Shipwrecked Sailor*. Translated by Randolph Hogan. New York: Knopf, 1986.

"García Márquez on Love, Plagues, and Politics." *New York Times Book Review*, February 21, 1988.

Hamill, Pete. "Love and Solitude." *Vanity Fair*, March 1988.

Janes, Regina. *One Hundred Years of Solitude: Modes of Reading*. Boston: G. K. Hall, 1990.

McMurray, George R. *Gabriel García Márquez*. New York: Ungar, 1977.

McNerney, Kathleen. *Gabriel García Márquez*. Columbia: University of South Carolina Press, 1989.

Minta, Stephen. *García Márquez: Writer of Colombia*. New York: Harper & Row, 1987.

Pearce, Jenny. *Colombia: Inside the Labyrinth*. London: Latin American Bureau, 1990.

Rodman, Selden. *Tongues of Fallen Angels*. New York: New Directions, 1974.

Simons, Marlise. "The Best Years of His Life: An Interview with Gabriel García Márquez." *New York Times Book Review*, April 10, 1988.

Stone, Peter H. "Gabriel García Márquez." *Paris Review* 82 (Winter 1981).

INDEX

SEAN DOLAN holds a degree in history and literature from the State University of New York. He is the author of several books for young adults, including biographies of *Christopher Columbus, Matthew Henson, and Junípero Serra.*

RODOLFO CARDONA is professor of Spanish and comparative literature at Boston University. A renowned scholar, he has written many works of criticism, including *Ramón, a Study of Gómez de la Serna and His Works and Visión del esperpento: Teoría y práctica del esperpento en Valle-Inclán.* Born in San José, Costa Rica, he earned his B.A. and M.A. from Louisiana State University and received a Ph.D. from the University of Washington. He has taught at Case Western Reserve University, the University of Pittsburgh, the University of Texas at Austin, the University of New Mexico, and Harvard University.

JAMES COCKCROFT is currently a visiting professor of Latin American and Caribbean studies at the State University of New York at Albany. A three-time Fulbright scholar, he earned a Ph.D. from Stanford University and has taught at the University of Massachusetts, the University of Vermont, and the University of Connecticut. He is the author or coauthor of numerous books on Latin American subjects, including *Neighbors in Turmoil: Latin America, The Hispanic Experience in the United States: Contemporary Issues and Perspectives, and Outlaws in the Promised Land: Mexican Immigrant Workers and America's Future.*